Landscapes of
MADEIRA

a countryside guide
Thirteenth edition

John and Pat Underwood

SUNFLOWER BOOKS

Thirteenth edition © 2017
Sunflower Books™
PO Box 36160
London SW7 3WS, UK
www.sunflowerbooks.co.uk

ISBN 978-1-85691-498-7

Levada do Furado (Walk 25)

Important note to the reader

We have tried to ensure that the descriptions and maps in this book are error-free at press date. ***Be sure to check our website for an 'Update' before you travel*** (see inside front cover). It is very helpful for us to receive your comments (sent in care of Sunflower Books, please) for the updating of future printings.

   We rely on those who use this book — especially walkers — to take along a good supply of common sense when they explore. Conditions change very rapidly on Madeira, and ***fires, storm damage or bulldozing may make a route unsafe at any time.*** If the route is not as we outline it here, and your way ahead is not secure, return to the point of departure. ***Never attempt to complete a tour or walk under hazardous conditions!*** Please read carefully the notes on pages 35 to 40, the Country code on page 8, and the introductory comments at the beginning of each tour and walk (regarding road conditions, equipment, grade, distances and time, etc). Explore ***safely***, while at the same time respecting the beauty of the countryside.

Cover photograph: Miradouro Ninho da Manta on the trail from Arieiro to Ruivo (Walk 19)
Title page: the high peaks from the ER228 near Rosário

Photographs: John Underwood, except for pages 13 (Conny Spelbrink), 126, 131 and cover (Shutterstock)
Maps: Sunflower Books, adapted from Portuguese IGC/military maps; see 'Acknowledgements', page 7
A CIP catalogue record for this book is available from the British Library.
Printed and bound in England: Short Run Press

Contents

3

4   Landscapes of Madeira

Pico Grande from the flanks of Pico do Arieiro

Preface

Again, many changes have come about since the last, greatly revised, edition of this book was published only two years ago. On the positive side, the road between Bica da Cana and Encumeada, closed on account of rockfall, has reopened. And there has been a good deal of regrowth after the fires in 2010/2012. *But* ... August 2016 saw more fires, fanned by gale-force winds. The devastation north of Funchal made the news throughout Europe, but the southern flanks of the Paúl da Serra weren't mentioned. Thankfully, the fires on the Paúl stayed south of the ER105; Rabaçal and the Janela Valley were not touched. So we have introduced a couple of new walks to compensate for routes lost to fire and lack of maintenance. Finally ... a great many road numbers have changed yet again!

Landscapes of Madeira has a long history. After we first published a small book of Madeira walks in 1980, it became the most widely used walkers' guide on the island and inspired a whole series of *Landscapes* books, which we publish under our Sunflower imprint. The aim of the series is to lead the visitor off the beaten track and into the countryside — whether by car, public transport, or (preferably) on foot. All Sunflower authors hope to convey more than mere enthusiasm for their chosen landscapes — love might be a better word.

The levadas

Our love affair with Madeira really came into blossom with our 'discovery' of the levadas. They never cease to fascinate or inspire us. No matter how tired we may be, to walk beside a levada always refreshes our spirits and brings the bounce back into our steps.

Whether you use this book to tour, walk or picnic, we will lead you along the levadas. Such watercourses are not unique to Madeira: what *is* unique is their **accessibility** and **extent**. You need only venture a little way off the main roads to begin to appreciate Madeira's myriad aqueducts — for their beauty, ingenuity of design, and for the courage and determination needed to bring the concept to its present glory. The island's irrigation system now comprises more than 2500km (1550 miles) of channels, including 50km (30 miles) of tunnels — and the work started centuries ago.

The earliest settlers on Madeira began cultivating the lower slopes in the south of the island, cutting out small terraces *(poios)* like those shown on page 7. Working with contractors (who sometimes used slave or convict labour), they built the

Tiny streams feed the Levada da Negra (Walk 2).

first small levadas, which carried water from springs higher up the mountainsides to irrigate their lands. These narrow watercourses (see left) plummet downhill, rushing and frothing with energy; their banks are often festooned with wild flowers.

By the early 1900s, there were about 200 of these levadas, meandering over about 1000km (620 miles). Many were privately owned, and the undisciplined appropriation of water meant that the island's most valuable asset was often unfairly distributed. In fact, by the mid 1930s, only two-thirds of the island's arable land was under cultivation — and just half of that was irrigated. Only the State had the money to implement a major building programme and the authority to enforce a more equitable system of distribution.

For there was plenty of water for irrigation, and torrents to spare for power. Clouds driven to the island by the prevailing northerly winds are caught by the central mountain chain, and as much as 2m (80 inches) of rain may fall in the north in a year, while the south coast may be almost dry for up to six months. In effect the island is a huge self-regulating reservoir. Rain seeps down into the porous volcanic ash but, on meeting impervious layers of rock, it wells up again in springs. Unless this rainwater is channelled, it just runs down ravines and into the sea.

In 1939 the Portuguese government sent a mission to the island to study an irrigation/hydroelectric scheme. The 'new' levadas created from its plans — wide mini-canals — contour through the valleys; their flow is stately and serene, and their banks are lovingly planted with agapanthus lilies and hydrangeas. These wide waterways are first channelled out at an altitude of about 1000m/3300ft, where the concentration of rainfall, dew and springs is greatest. The water is then piped down to the power stations lying just at the outer edge of the arable land (about 600m/2000ft), from where it flows on to the irrigated zones. Here, distribution is carried out by the *levadeiro*, who diverts the flow to each proprietor.

Terraces (poios) in the Ribeira dos Socorridos (Walk 1)

Although work is on-going, most of the mission's development plans were implemented by 1970. Among the most important projects were the Levada do Norte and the Levada dos Tornos, both of which you will discover as you tour, walk or picnic. Their incredible length, considering the terrain, is best gauged on the fold-out touring map. The work took only 25 years to complete, although it was all done by hand. How were the tunnels cut through the solid basalt? How did the workers channel out the levadas beneath the icy waterfalls, halfway between earth and sky? Often, as during the construction of the old corniche road ('Antiga 101'; see Car tour 5) between São Vicente and Porto Moniz, they were suspended from above in wicker baskets, while they fought the unyielding stone with picks. Many lost their lives to bring water and electricity to the islanders ... and unending joy to walkers.

Acknowledgements

We are very grateful for the invaluable help of everyone who contacts us with update suggestions and, of course, the Instituto Geográfico e Cadastral, for permission to adapt their maps. Special thanks to Conny Spelbrink who has rewalked several routes for recent editions.

Most of all, this book is dedicated to the memory of those who set us on our way and helped enormously with the first few editions: John and Richard Blandy, José Fernandes, Jim Leahy and Luís de Sousa.

Recommended reading

There are many good general guides available; check the publication date, because Madeira is still a dynamic 'work in progress'!.

Madeira: the discovery of the island by car and on foot by Raimundo Quintal (available on Madeira) will be of interest to all keen walkers who want to know more about the island's flora and ecology; it contains a wealth of background information for which there is no space in our book.

Madeira walk & eat (4th edition, Sunflower 2015) is our walking guide for short-break holidays, with 13 walks and two excursions. Eleven of the walks are in this book, and there are two new routes. The walk descriptions are complemented by information about restaurants and cafés en route, with their menus — and Madeiran recipes for you to cook at home.

Country code for walkers and motorists

The experienced rambler is used to following a 'country code', but the tourist out for a lark may unwittingly cause damage, harm animals, and even endanger his own life. Please respect this country code.

- **Only light fires at purpose-built fireplaces.**
- **Do not damage levadas.** Don't touch sluice gates or the stones used to control small sluices.
- **Protect all wild and cultivated plants.** Picking flowers or uprooting plants *is now illegal*. Never cross cultivated land!
- **Take all your litter away with you.**
- **Do not frighten animals.** They are not tame. By making loud noises, or trying to touch or photograph them, you may cause them to run in fear — over a precipice.
- **Leave all gates as you find them.** They have a purpose: generally to keep animals in — or out of — an area.
- **Walkers — DO NOT TAKE RISKS!** And remember:
— **At any time a walk may become unsafe.** If the route is not as we describe it, if mists are falling, or if it is late in the day, ***turn back!*** Remember, there is ***virtually no twilight on Madeira!***
— **NEVER walk alone** — and **always** tell a responsible person *exactly* where you are going and what time you plan to return.
— **Do not overestimate your capacity:** your speed will be determined by the slowest walker in the group, and bus connections may be vital.
— **Proper footwear is essential.** Flat clay paths can be deceptive; when they are damp they can be as slippery as ice.
— **Mists can fall suddenly** on the Paúl da Serra and in the mountains.
— **Warm clothing** and **extra rations** are needed in the mountains.
— **Compass, whistle, torch, first-aid kit and mobile phone** weigh little, but might save your life. In case of emergency, use your mobile to call 112 (the emergency number throughout the EU).
— **Protect yourself from the sun.**
— **A stout stick** is a help on steep terrain and to discourage the rare unfriendly dog (see also note on page 38, 'Nuisances').
— **Read and re-read the 'Important note'** on page 2 and guidelines on grade and equipment for each walk you plan to do.

Ancient laurels in the Fanal (Car tour 5, Walk and Picnic 36)

Getting about

There is no doubt that a **hired car** or taxi is the most convenient way of getting round the island. We hope that the liberal cross-references to picnics and walks in the touring section will inspire motorists and walkers to team up on hire. The walking maps show the car symbol (🚗) only at the *parking* places we recommend in the text; if friends can drop you off or collect you, look on the maps for places where roads cross the walks.

All **taxi** drivers carry a government-approved price list for journeys outside Funchal. Your hotel porter can suggest a driver for an all-day tour: many are knowledgeable about island culture and customs; some are even keen walkers!

Coach tours are the most popular way of 'seeing Madeira in a day'. They provide a painless introduction to road conditions and a remarkable overview of island scenery.

Since many of the best walks on Madeira are linear (see page 35), you will come to appreciate the **local interurban bus** network. The system is economical, reliable and safe. And you get great views perched up on the bus seats! The town plan on pages 10-11 shows you where to board your bus in Funchal; all depart from the Avenida do Mar. There are three main operators: Rodoeste (www.rodoeste.pt), SAM (www.sam.pt) and Horarios do Funchal (see 'town buses' below).

Orange town buses, as well as several key interurban routes, are operated by Horarios do Funchal. Their website (www.horariosdofunchal.pt) is just superb, with maps, routes, timetables and more. If convenient, *do* call at their office in Anadia Shopping (08.30-19.00 Mon-Fri only) if you have any questions or to buy city bus fare-saving tickets (see notes at the top of page 142). Otherwise, bus tickets are bought at the operators' kiosks near the relevant departure points, or on the bus itself (more expensive in the case of town buses).

Please do not rely *solely* on our **bus timetables** (pages 138-142). Download the latest timetables from the websites above and perhaps recheck times at the operators' stations or kiosks in Funchal. Unfortunately the Funchal Tourist Office no longer sells any bus timetable booklet, but some local tourist offices (eg at Santana, Ribeira Brava, Porto Moniz and Machico) may have lists of buses serving their areas.

Do arrive early! It may take you several minutes to find the bus you want, and they leave spot on time. On the road, it's always a good idea to *flag down* a bus, especially if there is no recognisable bus stop!

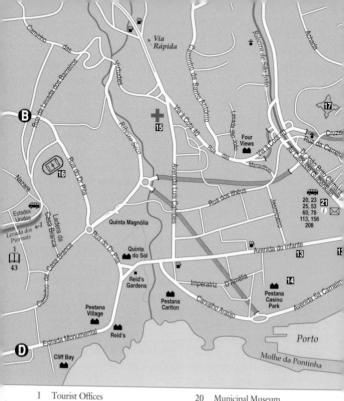

1   Tourist Offices
2   La Vie Funchal (Shopping Centre)
3   Boat Trips
4   Air Portugal (TAP)
5   Municipal Theatre
6   Casa do Turista
7   Government Offices
8   Sé (Cathedral)
9   Parliament (Old Customs House)
10 Praça da Autonomia/Forte San Felipe
11 Anadia Shopping, Horarios Office
12 Santa Caterina Chapel
13 Quinta Vigia (President's House)
14 Casino
15 Hospital
16 Barreiros Stadium
17 Forte do Pico
18 Quinta das Cruzes
19 Santa Clara Convent

20 Municipal Museum
21 Post Office, SAM Bus Station
22 São Lourenço Palace
23 Collegiate Church
24 Madeira Wine Institute
25 Law Courts
26 Town Hall
27 Museum of Sacred Art
28 New Customs House
29 Market
30 São Tiago Fort/Modern Art Museum
31 Madeira Story Centre
32 Livraria Esperanza (large bookshop)
33 Museum of Electricity
34 Embroidery Museum
35 Rodoeste Bus Station
36 EACL and Horarios Interurban Buses
37 Cable Car to Babosas and Car Park
38 Sugar Museum, Rodoeste (N° 50-52)

BUS DEPARTURES   (*i*: bus information kiosk, ticket sales)

N°	Destination	from	Company (and Livery)
2	Assomada	36	EACL (grey/red)
3	Estreito de Câmara de Lobos	9	Rodoeste (cream/red)*
4	Madalena do Mar	9	Rodoeste (cream/red)*
6	Arco de São Jorge via Encumeada	9	Rodoeste (cream/red)*
7	Ribeira Brava	9	Rodoeste (cream/red)*
20	Santo da Serra	*opposite* 9	SAM (white/cream/green)
23	Machico	*opposite* 9	SAM (white/cream/green)

*but their excursion buses to tourist destinations are *white*

10

Funchal

N°	Destination		from	Company (and Livery)
53	Faial	opposite	**9**	SAM (white/cream/green)
56	Santana via Faial		**36**	Horarios (white/yellow/silver)
60	Boqueirão	opposite	**9**	SAM (white/cream/green)
77	Santo da Serra		**36**	Horarios (white/yellow/silver)
78	Machico, Faial	opposite	**9**	SAM (white/cream/green)
80	Porto Moniz		**9**	Rodoeste (cream/red)*
81	Curral das Freiras		**36**	Horarios (white/yellow/silver)
96	Corticeiras		**9**	Rodoeste (cream/red)*
103	Arco de São Jorge via ER103		**36**	Horarios (white/yellow/silver)
110	Boqueirão via Caniço		**36**	Horarios (white/yellow/silver)
111	Achadinha		**36**	Horarios (white/yellow/silver)
113	Machico, Caniçal	opposite	**9**	SAM (white/cream/green)
114	Nogueira		**36**	Horarios (white/yellow/silver)
115	Estreito da Calheta		**9**	Rodoeste (cream/red)*
123	Campanário		**9**	Rodoeste (cream/red)*
129	Camacha		**36**	Horarios (white/yellow/silver)
138	São Jorge (Cabanas)		**36**	Horarios (white/yellow/silver)
139	Porto Moniz		**9**	Rodoeste (cream/red)*
142	Ponta do Pargo		**9**	Rodoeste (cream/red)*
148	Boa Morte		**9**	Rodoeste (cream/red)*
154	Cabo Girão		**9**	Rodoeste (cream/red)*
156/208	Machico, Maroços	opposite	**9**	SAM (white/cream/green)

ORANGE TOWN BUSES (Horarios do Funchal)

1	Lombada		**33**	22	Babosas	east of	**33**
2	Quebradas		**33**	29	Curral dos Romeiros	east of	**33**
3	Lombada	opposite	**6**	31	Jardim Botânico	opposite	**22**
8, 16	Santa Quitéria	east of	**28**	36, 37	Palheiro Ferreiro	east of	**33**
10A	Barreira	east of	**28**	45	Stadium	opposite	**6**
20, 21	Monte	northeast of	**33**	47	São João Latrão	east of	**33**

11

◉ Picnicking

In the course of some of our rambles we've come upon easy-to-reach picnic spots that might appeal to those of you who prefer *very* short walks. If you are car touring, they are an 'off-the-beaten-track' alternative to the island's many roadside picnic tables.

All the information you need to find these more secluded picnic spots is given below, where *picnic numbers correspond to walk numbers,* so that you can quickly find the general location on the island by looking at the touring map. We give you walking times and transport details. The location of the picnic is indicated by a green-printed symbol *P* on the corresponding *walking map,* which also shows the nearest 🚐 stop (if appropriate) and 🚗 car parking. Most picnic settings are illustrated.

Please remember to **wear sensible shoes and take a sunhat** (the symbol ○ after the title indicates a picnic **in full sun**). It's a good idea to take along a plastic groundsheet as well, in case it's damp or prickly.

If you are travelling by bus, check the latest schedules (see page 9). **Travelling by car**, park *well off* the road; *never* block a road or track. **All picnickers should read the Country code on page 8 and go quietly in the countryside**.

2 POÇO DA NEVE, ARIEIRO (map on reverse of touring map, photograph opposite) ○

🚗 ice house (Poço da Neve); it lies *below* the road, hidden by a stone wall edging a small parking bay, 2km below Pico do Arieiro (Car tours 1, 4). **Up to 5min on foot.** *Picnic by the ice house (no shade), or below it in the heath tree grove.* **Splendid view over moors, down to Funchal.**

3 EIRA DO SERRADO (map on reverse of touring map, photograph pages 46-47)

🚗 (Car tour 3) or 🚐 81 to the Eira do Serrado. **5min on foot.** *Follow Walk 3 (pages 47-48) from the 15min-point for five minutes.* **Fine view over Curral, away from the crowds.**

6 BOA MORTE (map pages 54-55, nearby photograph page 58)

🚗 or 🚐 127 to Boa Morte. By car, turn north off the ER229 0.5km west of Campanário for (among others) 'São Paulo, Boa Morte' (Car tour 6). Drive through two tunnels, ignoring a right turn to Lugar da Serra. Turn left at the roundabout at the end of the second tunnel, to cross the Levada do Norte immediately, and park nearby. **Up to 30min on foot.** By bus follow Short walk 6-3, page 55, returning on 🚐 148. **Up to 50min on foot.** *Pick up Walk 6 at the 4h35min-point and follow it for about 15 minutes.* **Fine views across and up the Ribeira Brava valley and to the Paúl da Serra. Sun or shade.**

12

The Santa Luzia Valley and Funchal from the Poço da Neve ('snow pit' or 'ice house'). Walk and Picnic 2; Car tours 1 and 4

7a PORTO NOVO FROM THE EAST (map pages 62-63)

🚗 or 🚌 60 (Boqueirão bus) to the Levada dos Tornos. **15-20min on foot.** By car, take the ER206 south from Águas Mansas (Car tour 2) and park by the levada, 1.6km downhill. By bus, ask the driver for 'Levada dos Tornos, Lombo Grande'; the levada is a minute uphill from the stop. *Head west on the levada: 10 minutes' walking will give you good views, or go as far as the tunnel with 'windows' (20min).* **This picnic overlooks the western side of the Porto Novo Valley and is at its best in spring. Some shade nearby.**

7b BOAVENTURA VALLEY (map pages 62-63, photo page 66)

🚗 or 🚌 as 7a above. **30min on foot.** *Follow Short walk 7-4, page 65.* **Overlook a golden valley (at its best in summer) and the south coast. Some shade.**

10 LEVADA DA SERRA (map pages 62-63, photograph page 21)

🚗 or 🚌 77 to the Sítio das Quatro Estradas, where the ER202 joins the ER110. By car, head west towards Poiso and park by the levada after 0.5km, just past the piggery (Car tours 2, 4). **7min on foot.** By bus, follow Short walk 10-4, page 71. **22min on foot.** *Head north on the levada for about seven minutes.* **No far-reaching views, just a lovely setting.**

11 LEVADA DO CANIÇAL (map pages 80-81)

🚗 (Car tour 2) or 🚌 113 to the 'Pico do Facho' bus stop. Motorists should park at the start of the road to Pico do Facho, well tucked in. **20-30min on foot.** *Follow Short walk 11, page 72, for only 20-30min.* **Picnic on grassy verges in full sun, or in the shade of mimosas.**

13 ABRA BAY (map pages 76-7, photos overleaf and page 78) ○

🚗 (Car tour 2) or 🚌 113 to the Abra Bay viewpoint (🅿) on São Lourenço Point, at the end of the ER214. **Up to 20min on foot.** *Picnic at the viewpoint or follow Walk 13 (page 76) for 15-20min.* **Magnificent coastal views, but no shade.**

15 PORTELA (map pages 80-81, photograph pages 82-83)

🚗 (Car tour 4) or 🚌 53 or 78 to Portela. **5min on foot.** *Follow Walk 15 (page 83) for 5min; if you like, continue further east along the track.* **Superb view over Penha de Aguia, away from the coaches. Shade.**

16 LEVADA DO CASTELEJO (map pages 80-81, photo pages 84-85)

🚐 (Car tour 4) or 🚌 53 or 78 to Cruz. **Up to 30min on foot.** *Follow Walk 16 (page 84).* **You can look out towards Penha de Águia (20min) or up to the high peaks (25-30min). Shade nearby.**

19 PICO DO ARIEIRO (map on reverse of touring map, photograph pages 90-91) ○

🚐 Pico do Arieiro (Car tours 1, 4). **Up to 15min on foot.** *Picnic near the start of Walk 19, on a grassy verge before the first viewpoint (notes page 90).* **Stupendous mountain setting and views. No shade.**

20 ACHADA DO TEIXEIRA (map on reverse of touring map, photograph page 93)

🚐 Achada do Teixeira (Car tour 4). **5-50min on foot.** *Picnic at Homem em Pé (the basaltic dyke just below the house; 5min; shade), or follow Short walk 20 (page 92) to picnic on the Ruivo path or at Pico Ruivo itself (50min).* **Lacks the drama of Picnic 19, but the settings and views are fabulous.**

These rocks off the north coast of the Ponta de São Lourenço seem almost fluorescent (Car tour 2, Walk and Picnic 13)

22 QUEIMADAS (map pages 98-99, photograph page 97)

⌂ Queimadas Park (accessible via a narrow lane) or Pico das Pedras on the ER218: see Car tour 4, pages 27-28. **Up to 35min on foot.** *Picnic by the Queimadas houses, or explore the Levada do Caldeirão Verde (see Short walks, page 97).* **No far-reaching views, but a fairy tale setting.**

25 BALCÕES (map page 105)

⌂ (Car tours 1, 4) or 🚌 56, 103 or 138 to Ribeiro Frio. **25min on foot.** *Follow the Short walk on page 104.* **Superb outlook over the central peaks, the Metade Valley and Fajã da Nogueira. Shade, bar-café nearby.**

26 PICO DA BONECA (map pages 98-99)

⌂ or 🚌 56, 103 or 138 to Cortado, just east of Santana (Car tours 1, 4). **25-30min on foot.** *Follow Short walk 1 on page 107; picnic at the trig point or on the contouring return path.* **Superb views over Santana and Faial. Adequate shade.**

27 ARCO DE SÃO JORGE (map page 110, photograph page 29)

⌂ (Car tours 1, 4) or 🚌 6 or 103 to the Snack Bar Arco on the ER211. **10-15min on foot.** *Take the beautifully cobbled trail at the left of the snack bar and follow it as long as you like.* **Brilliant views towards Boaventura and down over the sea from a sugar-loaf cliff.**

31 LOMBO DO MOURO (map on reverse of touring map, photos page 116).

⌂ to the parking bay above the Lombo do Mouro house on the ER105 between Encumeada and Bica da Cana (Car tour 5) — not currently signposted; see access notes on page 115. **10-15min on foot.** *Descend the steps to the levada, just before the house, then turn right.* **Superb views east to the peaks and west to the escarpment of the Paúl da Serra; rushing levada; nearby shade.**

32 LEVADA DO NORTE, ENCUMEADA (map on reverse of touring map, nearby photograph page 117, right)

⌂ or 🚌 6 to Encumeada. Park at the viewpoint on the north side of the pass (Car tours 1, 5). **5-15min on foot.** *Climb steps opposite the bar/restaurant on the south side of the pass, to join the Levada do Norte (signposted 'Folhadal'). Picnic anywhere beside the levada, before the first tunnel (14min).* **Wonderful views to the great peaks; wealth of vegetation on the levada. Shade nearby.**

33 BICA DA CANA (map on reverse of touring map, photograph page 119)

⌂ at the entrance drive (with two concrete pillars) to the house (Car tour 5). **Up to 10min on foot.** *Follow the track towards the Bica house and then up to the triangulation point/miradouro (no shade).* **Stupendous views to the great peaks. Plenty of shade in the surrounding area.**

34 NOSSA SENHORA DA BOA MORTE (map page 120)

⌂ at the chapel (a detour on Car tour 6). **No walking or up to 20min on foot.** *Picnic just below the chapel, on grassy slopes, or walk on to Pico Vermelho (see map page 120).* **Idyllic settings in a little-visited corner of the island.**

36 FANAL (map page 125, photographs pages 4 and 126)

🚌 Fanal forestry house, off the ER209 (Car tour 5). **5min-1h on foot.** *Picnic just near the forestry house (there are some tables, benches and barbecues) or follow Walk 36 on page 127 as long as you like. Brilliant views over the Ribeira da Janela and Seixal valleys. Wonderland of ancient laurels for shade.*

37a-e RABAÇAL (map pages 124-125, photograph page 129)

🚌 Rabaçal (Car tour 5). See parking options on page 128. If you park at the barbecue building on the ER211, you can walk to Rabaçal in 30 minutes: see Alternative walk 37-1, page 128; *torch essential.* **No walking, or up to 50min on foot** *from Rabaçal.* *There are four picnic choices: (a) by the Rabaçal houses; (b) a sun-trap below the houses, at the Rabaçal end of the tunnel (follow Short walk 37-2 down to the Levada das 25 Fontes and turn left); (c) Risco waterfall (Short walk 37-1); (d) 25 Fontes (Short walk 37-2). All these settings are lovely and have ample shade.*

38 LEVADA DO ALECRIM (map pages 124-125)

🚌 at the parking area on the ER105, at the top of the road to Rabaçal (Car tour 5). **12min on foot.** *Follow Walk 38 (page 131) to the pretty little reservoir. No views, but a lovely shady setting on a hot day.*

39 FONTE RUIVAS, BELOW PICO RUIVO DO PAÚL (map pages 124-125, photographs page 132)

🚌 at the junction of the ER105 to Bica da Cana and the road to Estanquinhos, by a small levada (Car tour 5). **Up to 20min on foot.** *Follow Walk 39 (page 132) for as long as you like. Beautiful views across the Paúl da Serra and its miniature 'red peak'. Plenty of shade.*

40 PRAZERES (map pages 134-135, photograph below)

🚌 or 🚌 80 or 142 to Prazeres. By car (detour on Car tour 6), park at the Hotel Jardim Atlántico. **10min on foot.** By bus, walk 2km down to the hotel. **40min on foot.** *Follow Walk 40 (page 133) for just over 10min. Dramatic views to the sea and steeply terraced cliffs shown below.*

42 LEVADA ABOVE RIBEIRA DA JANELA (map page 137, photograph page 136)

🚌 or 🚌 80 to the levada (Car tour 5). See 'How to get there', page 136. **Up to 30min on foot.** *Follow Walk 42 (page 137) as long as you like. Fantastic views to the great Janela Valley; picturesque levada; some picnic tables. Good shade.*

From a pine-shaded bench below Prazeres, you look out towards some of the most fascinating coastal cliffs on the island (Walk and Picnic 40, detour on Car tour 6).

☀ *Touring* ————

Getting around the island is a real pleasure for us, thanks to the new roads and expressways. From Funchal we can now be on the Paúl da Serra in 45 minutes — a drive that used to take three hours!

You may find some of our car tours 'slow going'; remember, you can always cut them short by picking up one of the fast roads; the only price to be paid is that you won't see a thing from the inside of the endless tunnels.

Drive *patiently;* off the expressways you are unlikely to average more than 20-30km/h. On the older roads *beware of potholes and, sometimes, very deep ditches (some of which double as levadas) at the sides, remembering that your hire car insurance does not cover damage to tyres.* Plan leisurely excursions if possible, with walking breaks to stretch your legs. **The best one-day excursion is Car tour 1; Car tours 4 and 5 make an ideal two-day programme.**

In the touring and walking notes we often refer to **road numbers**. *This is to help you with orientation when using our maps,* since at time of writing only the express roads are numbered, although this may change in the future.

Our touring notes are brief: they include little history or information that can be found in general guides. We concentrate instead on the 'logistics' of touring: times and distances, road conditions, getting to the best viewpoints at the right time of day, etc. Most of all, we emphasise possibilities for **walking** and **picnicking**. If you're picnicking or sharing a car with walkers, you should find the ⊖ symbols on the walking maps useful: these alert you to places where you can park near a walk. And *do* refer to these walking maps from time to time while touring — perhaps when you stop at a viewpoint; they contain far more information than the touring map.

The large fold-out touring map is designed to be held out opposite the touring notes. City exits correspond to those on the Funchal plan on pages 10-11. **Symbols** used in the text are explained in the map key; note that only *isolated* hotels and restaurants are highlighted, since you will find these facilities, as well as medical centres, in all major villages.

Allow ample time for stops: our times include only short breaks at viewpoints labelled ⊡ in the notes. Calculate time for **detours** as well: places, picnics and walks shown in ( ) are only accessible via detours off the main route.

All motorists should read the Country code on page 8 and go quietly in the countryside. *Boa viagem!*

Car tour 1: MADEIRA NORTH AND SOUTH

Funchal • Encumeada • São Vicente • (Porto Moniz) • Boaventura • Santana • Faial • Ribeiro Frio • Poiso • (Pico do Arieiro) • Monte • Funchal

113km/70mi; 5-6 hours' driving ***without detours*** *(add about 30km/ 19mi; 1h for the detour to Porto Moniz and 14km/9mi; 1h for the detour to Pico do Arieiro); take the nearest expressway exit from Funchal.*

On route: ⊓ around Vinháticos, Encumeada, Chão dos Louros, above Rosário, Feiteiras, Ponta Delgada, Boaventura, São Jorge, ER103 around Ribeiro Frio, Poiso, Pico do Arieiro; Picnics (see ***P*** symbol and pages 12-16): (2, 19, 22), 25, 26, 27, 32, (42); Walks (2), 5, (7), 8, 10, 18, 20, 21, 22, (23, 24), 25, 26, 27, (28, 29), 31, 32, (42)

If you have only one day to tour the island, then this is the circuit to do, ***including the detours to Porto Moniz and Pico do Arieiro****. Leave Funchal* ***very*** *early in the morning; we've planned the tour so that you have the best views west in the morning and east in the afternoon. If, however, you have a car for several days, then do Car tours 4 and 5* ***instead*** *of this long expedition. The roads are fair to good, but a short stretch on the north coast east of Ponta Delgada is very narrow and you may have to back up to let oncoming traffic pass (to avoid this, turn right towards 'Lombada' at the first crossroads past the 'Ponta Delgada' sign).*

From Funchal take the expressway west (Via Rápida; VR1), quickly whizzing across the lovely 'winged' bridge over the Socorridos. Not far beyond the exit for Cabo Girão/ Quinta Grande the road dives beneath Campanário's church in a tunnel and soon describes a breathtaking arc out over the coast on a long bridge. After Exit 2 for Campanário and a short tunnel you enter the final, long tunnel: keep in the *left-hand* lane as you near the end of it, to follow signposting for 'São Vicente' (17km).

After a fairly straight run along a narrow canyon graced with poplars you come to a fork: keep left for 'S Vicente via Encumeada' (22km). Now the road begins its winding ascent in earnest. Beyond **Serra de Água** you pass several picnic areas (📷⊓) and then the Pousada dos Vinháticos (▲📷⊓), beautifully sited below a ridge — the aptly named Crista de Galo ('Cock's Comb'). Some 2.5km further uphill (past the Residencial Encumeada ▲), Walk 4 comes in along a track on the right. The snaking ascent ends at **Encumeada★**, just at the centre of the island (1004m/3293ft; 28km ✕). Park on the left at the far side of this pass (📷⊓WC), from where there are spectacular views down to the north coast and up to the Paúl da Serra in the west and the high peaks to the east. Walk 31 can begin here; Walk 20 ends on the other side of the road. While you are here, *do* take the opportunity to see the great Levada do Norte, described on pages 117-118 (Walk 32 and ***P***32); the steps are on the south side of the pass, opposite the bar/restaurant.

Then descend into São Vicente's welcoming valley (📷⊓), past **Chão dos Louros**, a lovely laurel grove (⊓ with fire-

Car tours 1 and 5, Walk 29: The graceful clock tower of Nossa Senhora de Fátima crowns a hilltop in São Vicente's valley.

places). Soon you'll have good views (📷🍴) over Rosário's church and stream: in high summer the hayricks weave ribbons of gold into the tapestry of this emerald landscape. Beyond **Rosário** you find yourself in the settings shown above and on page 1. At a roundabout, ignore the first exit signed to São Vicente (via a tunnel); take the second exit, to stay on the old road. At **Feiteiras** (📷🍴) you pass the ER208 to 'Ginjas' and 'Lanço'. Walk 29 begins and ends 5km up this road, at the Levada da Fajã do Rodrigues.

There is ample parking to the right of the carefully restored nucleus of **São Vicente** (39km ☥∩), a good place to take a break for morning coffee ... and to make a decision: are you going to try to fit in a detour to Porto Moniz? If it's now later than 10.00, you really don't have the time. If you *do* have time, use the notes for Car tour 5 on page 30.

At the roundabout as you leave São Vicente (🚰), ignore the left turn signed to Porto Moniz; go straight ahead towards the chapel (☥) built into a hollowed-out rock south of the lavender, modernistic bridge. Then either turn left towards Porto Moniz or follow the main tour: turn right on the coastal ER211. After passing through a tunnel, your attention will be drawn to the chequered pattern made by the heath tree hedges protecting the terraces from the fierce northerly winds. Most of the fields are planted with vines, but this is for table wine; the vines which yield the grapes for the fortified Madeira wines are grown in the south, around Estreito de Câmara de Lobos. You skirt above the lava-fertile promontory of **Ponta Delgada** (46km 🚰) and soar up to a viewpoint (📷🍴) over the village setting and headlands to the east.

Beyond Ponta Delgada, a short stretch of cobbled road in the shadow of menacing cliffs and an old, narrow tunnel are a delightful reminder of bygone days, when driving round the island was a spine-rattling experience. Then the road turns inland, leaving the awesome coast for the green-gold gentleness of the great **Boaventura** (49km) valley. Walk 27a ends at the village church; Walk 27b begins there. Just past Boaventura there is a good viewpoint (📷🅿) on the left. At the head of the valley (🅿) a road may one day be built to Curral das Freiras, via Falca.

As the road returns to the coastal cliffs, the Snack Bar/Restaurante Arco (*P27*), on the left, marks the halfway point of spectacular Walk 27b. You pass above **Arco de São Jorge** (56km), decked out with vines and hedgerows and rainbows of flowers. The hillsides are cultivated almost down to the sea, along the sweeping curve (*arco*) of the bay. Climb past mossy cliffs and dark pines brightened by banks of agapanthus, to another *miradouro* (📷🅿) with fine views back to Ponta Delgada. Adjacent to this viewpoint are the beautifully landscaped Cabanas rondavels (🔺🍴).

Soon turn left for 'Vigia'. Take the short detour left to the *vigia* (📷), an old whalers' look-out. Then return and take the first left, to continue into **São Jorge** (67km 🍴🅿). The richest baroque church outside Funchal is on your right. Turn left on rejoining the ER211: beyond a road north to the Calhau lido (Walk 18) and a bridge, you pass a road up right to Ilha, where Walk 28 ends. Beyond a couple of tunnels, at a roundabout, turn right into **Santana**★ (75km *i*🅿🚻*P26*), a market garden centre with a theme park of island culture. Walk 26 is a lovely countryside circuit around Santana. If you haven't brought a picnic, this is the best place to stop for lunch.

From Santana we take the *old road* to **Faial** and then the ER103 as far as Poiso; use the notes on pages 28 and 29 (Car tour 4). It's about two hours from Santana to Funchal and, hopefully, you will have time to walk to Balcões from **Ribeiro Frio** (Short walk 25) and drive to Arieiro from Poiso.

Past **Poiso** (100km *excluding* the detour to Arieiro), continue south to the signposted car park for **Monte**★ (108km 🚻✿), 300m above the village. Walk above the pretty gardens to the church of Our Lady of the Mount, where you can see the tiny poignant statue to Madeira's patron saint. From the bottom of the church steps (departure point for the famous toboggan rides), you could follow the agapanthus-banked lane to the left (past the Monte Palace Gardens ✿ and Funchal cable car terminus; 🚡), to Babosas Balcony (15 minutes return on foot; 📷🚡). Here you'll find a fine viewpoint over the impressive bowl of Curral dos Romeiros in the João Gomes River valley, and there is another cable car down to the Jardim Botânico. Walk 8 begins here; Walk 7 could begin here.

Now it's just 5km back to Funchal (113km).

Car tour 2: EASTERN MADEIRA'S GENTLE CHARMS

Funchal • Camacha • Santo da Serra • Machico • Ponta de São Lourenço • Pico do Facho • Santa Cruz • Funchal

85km/53mi; 4 hours' driving; Exit A from Funchal (plan pages 10-11)

On route: ⊼ at São Lourenço Point, Santa Cruz; Picnics (see *P* symbol and pages 12-16): (7a-b), (8), (10), 11, 13; Walks 7-14

Some of the old roads are potholed and have deep ditches at the sides. Allow a full day, to make the most of São Lourenço Point.

Either follow 'Camacha' off the Via Rápida (Exit 13) or leave Funchal from Exit A (Rua Dr Manuel Pestana Júnior). In either case, keep following signs for Camacha. Just 200m beyond a sign indicating a right turn to 'S Gonçalo 2km' you pass a fairly large large electricity sub-station on your right: the road to the **Palheiro Gardens** (❀↓) is at the far side of the sub-station fence. Just 1km above the Palheiro

Levada da Serra (Picnic 10 and Walk 10)

junction, the ER205 crosses the Levada dos Tornos (Walk
7). Now the road runs below the Levada da Serra (Walk 10),
which may be joined at various points. Continue (🚗) up to
Camacha★ (10km 🚌🍴WC), the centre of Madeira's willow-
craft industry. The village square, the Achada da Camacha,
overlooks the magnificent Porto Novo Valley. Short walk 7-3
begins here in the square.

Follow the one-way system out of the square, then turn
right (signposted to 'Rochão' and 'Santo António da Serra').
Beyond **Eira de Fora** you come to **Águas Mansas** (15km)
and pass the junction of the ER206 south (***P**7a-b; photograph
page 66). Access to Short walk 10-3 is via the road on your
left, 100m past this turn-off. Then round a bend to enter the
great Boaventura basin, another valley irrigated by the Levada
dos Tornos. At 19km pass the ER202 left to Poiso; our
favourite stretch of the Levada da Serra begins not far up this
road (***P**10; photograph page 21) and would take you to
Portela (Short walk 10-4, followed by Short walk 10-5).

At 21km fork right into **Santo da Serra** (22km ❀🚌), a
wooded village with several fine *quintas*. Walk 9 begins and
ends here; Walk 10 could as well. Beyond the church, ignore
the first sharp left turn to Machico, but bear left at a Y-fork
signposted to Santa Cruz; you skirt the golf course (⛳). At a
fork past the clubhouse, turn left for 'Machico' and continue
downhill, in 0.6km passing a right turn to Água de Pena and
the Capela dos Cardais, where Walk 9 can also start. Two
viewpoints (📷) on this road afford superb perspectives on
the flawless setting of emerald-green Machico Bay, Pico do
Facho, and the sun-baked arm of São Lourenço Point.

From the second viewpoint, continue down to the coast
road and go left for **Machico★** (30km *i*❀🚌), Madeira's first
settlement. Of particular interest are the Manueline church
and the Chapel of Miracles. The latter, on the east side of the
river, was founded in 1420 on the site of Zarco's first landfall;
destroyed by a flood in 1803, the chapel was rebuilt later in
the 19th century.

Leave Machico following 'Caniçal ER109', *not* 'Porto da
Cruz, Santana'. After climbing the lush eastern flanks of
Machico's valley, you come to a turn-off right to **Pico do
Facho** (33km), where Walk 12 begins. Drive up to this small
peak (📷), to admire the view over Machico and its harbour,
nestling below the hills of Santo da Serra. Descending from
the viewpoint, turn right into the old Caniçal tunnel (***P**11),
where Walk 11 ends; Walk 14 and Short walk 11 begin here.
Beyond a pretty line of palm trees fanning out above the grassy
slopes, turn down right into **Caniçal** (40km; whaling **M**), a
once-poor fishing port now bursting its seams with new
buildings as a result of the tax-free industrial zone.

There are superb views over the Bay of Funchal from Pináculo, an aloe-spiked promontory above São Gonçalo. What a stupendous view of the fireworks the nearby hotel must have on New Year's Eve!

From here return to the main ER214 and continue straight out (▲✕) to **São Lourenço Point★**. You'll pass parking for Praínha, a black sand beach, and then Quinta do Lorde, a gated resort so large it even has its own church and marina. It has been beautifully designed and built, but reports vary: will it last or go bankrupt out in this isolated location? It's rather like a ghost town, with few people about.

When you reach the end of the point, use the notes on pages 76-78 to explore; perhaps picnic at Abra Bay (46km ⊚⟠*P*13; Walk 13) or one of the viewpoints (⊚⟠).

On your return from the point, join the expressway at the roundabout by turning right into the tunnel. This road will whisk you quickly back to Funchal, but we suggest at least one more stop: turn off at Exit 21 for 'Santa Cruz (este)'. Coming onto the old coastal road, keep on into delightful **Santa Cruz★** (62km ♦⟠). Here you can stretch your legs in the *til*-shaded square and visit the bright-white church of São Salvador, one of the finest Manueline buildings on the island and the largest church outside Funchal. The lido, with its cafés, palms and pebble beach, is a pleasant place to relax. There is also a water park (on the west side of the village).

Leaving Santa Cruz, rejoin the Via Rápida. Exit 16 would take you to **Caniço** (*i*♦⟐), a major tourist centre. If you have the time, you could return to Funchal via the viewpoint shown above: from Caniço's attractive church, it's just a short way up to the old road (ER204). Follow this west towards Funchal, quickly coming to Cancela. From here *carefully follow signposting to São Gonçalo*, to join the narrow old road hugging the coast *(ignore the turn-off for the Via Rápida)*. Some 2km along pull over left at the viewpoint, then return via São Gonçalo to Funchal centre (about 85km, depending on detours).

Car tour 3: THE CORRAL AND THE CAPE

Funchal • Pico dos Barcelos • Eira do Serrado • Curral das Freiras • Câmara de Lobos • Cabo Girão • Funchal

64km/40mi; 3 hours' driving; Exit B from Funchal (plan pages 10-11)

On route: ⊼ on the ER107 to Curral; Picnic (see *P* symbol and pages 12-16): 3; Walks 3, (4, 6). (Walk 1 is near this tour, but is best reached direct from Funchal by bus.)

For the best light, do this short tour in the afternoon. The approach to Curral das Freiras is now via a tunnel; the narrow old road is closed.

Either take Exit 8 for 'P dos Barcelos' off the Via Rápida or leave Funchal by Exit B (the statue to Freedom in front of Reid's Gardens, signposted 'Estádio'). Leaving from Exit B, you very soon pick up signposting for Pico dos Barcelos. As you approach the slender spire of São Martinho's church, on a hill, turn right, cross the expressway, and continue to **Pico dos Barcelos★** (6km 🚻WC), a tree-shaded *miradouro* offering fine views over Funchal and the east.

Continue north, now following signposting to the Eira do Serrado. The ER107 climbs through forests of eucalyptus and pine splintered by golden sun-shafts (✕⊼). Ignore the tunnel to Curral and then a road to Pico do Arieiro, both on the right. (The latter, only open from 9.30 to 17.30 or 19.00 in summer, crosses Walk 2 higher up and emerges near the ice house where Walk 2 begins.) A good viewpoint (🖼) over the Socorridos ravine is passed on the left, before the road curves right to the **Eira do Serrado★** (18km 🏨✕🖼 WC*P*3). No doubt you will join the crowds and climb the paved path to the main viewpoint, from where there are stupendous views over Curral, 400m/ 1300ft below. But to hug all this splendour to yourself, follow Walk 3 from the 15min-point (page 47) for five to ten minutes.

Beyond the Eira the old road to Curral ('Antiga 107') is closed. Drive back to the tunnel and continue down into the crater-like ravine where **Curral das Freiras★** (the 'Nuns' Corral'; 22km WC; photograph pages 46-47) huddles below awesome heights. Curral is a famous walkers' 'crossroads': Walks 3 and Alternative walk 20 end near the village, and experts could begin or end Walk 4 here. One day they may build a tunnel from Curral to Boaventura in the north.

Return the same way (via the long tunnel) and, 1km past Pico dos Barcelos (just before São Martinho Church), turn right, to get on the expressway west. After crossing the Socorridos, take Exit 5 for **Câmara de Lobos★** (*i* and ✝ founded by Zarco in 1424). Follow the one-way system down to the centre. When you've looked at the stark new esplanade, the colourful fishing boats and the church, leave on the road signposted 'CTT Correos'. As you make the sharp left turn back to the main ER229 (🚍), a plaque above a terrace on the right alerts you to the place where Sir Winston Churchill

From the top of Cabo Girão, safe behind iron railings, you can marvel at the toy ships at sea some 580m/1900ft below you ... and at the tenacity of the sure-footed Madeiran farmers working their tiny terraces.

painted the curving white arc of the village against the backdrop of the awesome red cape, Cabo Girão. Heading back west on the ER229 (🚌), turn right after just over 1.5km, to **Pico da Torre** (📷), a fine viewpoint over Câmara de Lobos.

The road winds below **Estreito de Câmara de Lobos** (44km), where the grapes for the island's fortified wines are grown*, and an exceptionally gorgeous display of terraced vineyards pours down the hillsides below **Garachico**'s church (photograph page 57).** Turn left to **Cabo Girão★** (51km *i*📷🚻WC), where Short walk 6-1 can end. From this sea-cliff you enjoy the spectacular view shown above. But if you are a keen walker, your eyes will be drawn to the 'winged' bridge over the Socorridos and then up the valley to the mountains.

From here return to Funchal on the expressway (64km).

*__Detour 1__ (either 8.5 or 14km return; see map pages 54-55): Turn right into Estreito, curl left round the church, then drive straight uphill (sign: Jardim da Serra). Just beyond a chapel on the left (0.7km past the church), you cross the Levada do Norte (Walk 6). At a fork (1.6km) keep left for 'Foro'. Ignore a road on the right (3.4km) and curve round left over a bridge. Almost immediately, bear right at a Y-fork for 'Boca da Corrida', ignoring the hotel signposted to the left. This area is called **Jardim da Serra** (Garden in the Mountains). The garish hotel you pass on the left (4.2km; 🏨✕) was once a lovely old *quinta,* built in the 1800s by the English consul, Henry Veitch. From here he sent fruit, books and old wines to Napoleon, when the Northumberland anchored in Funchal on its passage to St Helena. From the hotel you can continue uphill for another 2.5km to the end of the road: **Boca da Corrida**, the superb viewpoint where Walk 4 begins and Alternative walk 5 nears its end.

**__Detour 2__ (8km return): Just after Garachico you pass a road off left to the Via Rápida. You can follow this road all the way to the coastal cliffs, where there is a cable car down to Fajã das Bebras, a landslip just east of Cabo Girão. As you approach Junction 4 of the Via Rápida, a brown sign *('Fajãs do Cabo Girão')* points the way. Map pages 54-55.

Car tour 4: MOUNTAINS AND MORE MOUNTAINS!

Funchal • Poiso • Pico do Arieiro • Portela • Porto da Cruz • Achada do Teixeira • Santana • (São Jorge • Arco de São Jorge) • Faial • Ribeiro Frio • Funchal

*143km/89mi; about 6-7 hours' driving, **excluding** the detour to Arco de São Jorge; Exit A from Funchal (plan pages 10-11)*

On route: ㅈ at Poiso, Pico do Arieiro, ER202 west of the Levada da Serra, ER110 north of Portela, ER103 around Ribeiro Frio, Pico das Pedras, ER218 to Achada do Teixeira, path to Pico Ruivo, Queimadas Park; Picnics (see **P** symbol and pages 12-16): 2, 10, 15, 16, 19, 20, (22), 25, 26, (27); Walks: 2, 7, 9, 10, 14-21, (22-24), 25, 26, (28)

*It is usual to include the mountainous northeast of the island in what is often called a 'Santana Tour', covering all of central Madeira (our Car tour 1). We find this very hectic and urge you to devote an entire day to visiting the great rugged peaks and the gentle moorland roads radiating from Poiso Pass. This tour fits in nicely with Car tour 5, providing a leisurely two-day introduction to many of Madeira's best landscapes. Start out early in the morning and **aim to reach Arieiro no later than 09.30**; clouds often descend by about 10.00. If you do not plan to take any short walks, you will have time to go further west than Santana — to São Jorge (18km return; 1h) or possibly Arco (38km return; 2h) — a part of the island not to be missed. Roads are fair to good: winding and sometimes badly surfaced due to heavy rainfall (especially the ER218 to Achada do Teixeira).*

The direct route to Arieiro from Funchal is Exit C (Rua 31 de Janeiro; ER103), via Monte. But we suggest you try another way: leave as for Car tour 2 and use the notes on page 21 past the road to the **Palheiro Gardens** (5km). In a minute more, the ER201 joins from the left. Turn up left here and follow this pine- and eucalyptus-shaded road northwest. You cross the Levada dos Tornos (Walk 7) and pass the cobbled trail where Walk 10 begins. Some 2.7km further on, there is a fine *miradouro* on the left, looking out over Curral dos Romeiros. At **Terreiro da Luta★** (14km †✗️WC) a statue to Our Lady of Peace commemorates the sufferings of the people of Funchal during World War I. At the base of the statue there is a rosary made from the anchor chains of ships torpedoed in Funchal harbour. In the early 1900s a luxurious cog railway climbed up here via Monte; there are now plans for an electric version starting from Monte. The views over the city's setting are superb, but soon you must press on! Join the ER103 ahead and turn right.* The road, lined with hydrangeas and agapanthus, snakes its way up through the desolation of the (in 2010) fire-ravaged Funchal Ecological Park to **Poiso Pass** (1400m/4600ft; 20km ✗️🅿️).

*Some 3km beyond Terreiro da Luta, you pass two roads on the left. The first goes to a viewpoint at Pico Alto (🅿️) and the second (open daily 08.00-19.00) climbs all the way to the Pico do Arieiro road. But you *cannot* get to Arieiro this way (there is a cul-de-sac sign at the entrance); a locked gate bars access to the ER202. But *do* explore this forestry road (🅿️) if you have time. A short way further north on the ER103 is the Parque Ecológico Information Centre (ℹ️).

Here turn left on the highland road (ER202) to **Pico do Arieiro★** (1818m/5963ft; 27km ⌖🅿︎✕WC*P*19), with its NATO radar station and large café/restaurant. Walk 19, the island's 'classic' route between the highest peaks, begins from the viewpoint here, in the wonderful setting shown on pages 90-91 and the cover).

On your return, watch for the ice house hidden below the road on your right, some 2km below the peak ('Poço da Neve'; *P*2; photograph page 13). Walk 2 starts here. You pass a road off right to the Eira do Serrado (open from 09.30 to 17.30 or 19.00 in summer) and then the meteorological station. Once back at **Poiso** (34km), go straight ahead on the ER202 opposite, a beautiful moorland road. Overlooking the reservoir (*lagoa*) near Santo da Serra, you descend past shaded 🅰︎ and cross the Levada da Serra (*P*10; photograph page 21). You meet the ER110 at the Sítio das Quatro Estradas ('the four roads'; 42km); Short walk 10-3 ends here; Short walk 10-4 begins here. Turn left, passing the road into Santo da Serra (🚍) and continuing north to **Portela★** (49km ✕⌖*P*15), where Walk 25 ends and Walk 15 begins. Here you enjoy the superb view to the north coast shown on pages 82-83, with Penha de Águia dominating the landscape.

From Portela take the ER110 north (⌖🅰︎). Alternative walk 16, through a valley called 'Hold on; watch you don't fall!', begins at **Referta** (52.5km). At a roundabout, be sure to take the first right to **Porto da Cruz** (55km 🚍), where Walks 14 and 15 end. Continue on the ER110, passing a good viewpoint (⌖) back over the village as you climb west to skirt the towering mass of Eagle Rock. Don't blink, or you might miss **Cruz** (57km; *P*16), where Walk 16 begins and the descent from Eagle Rock ends (Walk 17). Just before crossing the bridge over the Ribeira de São Roque, turn right (signposted '**Penha de Águia**'). Walk 17 begins 1.1km uphill, at the Restaurante Galé (✕). Continue to a turning circle at the end of the road, from where there is a fine view (⌖) towards Faial and up to Pico do Arieiro. Return, cross the bridge and pass the ER103 on your left (60km ✕). Go over a second bridge and perhaps turn left at the sign 'Zona balnear', to visit **Faial**'s pretty lido, edged with basalt prisms. Return and, at the roundabout, turn right for 'Faial, Antiga ER', ignoring the expressway tunnel. Skirt the centre of Faial and make for Santana — for the present ignoring the two roadside viewpoints. The sun is now too high for this landscape to be seen at its best.

With good planning you will reach the Santana area late in the morning. Just past the petrol station on the left, turn left on the ER218 for 'Pico das Pedras/Pico Ruivo'. Climb to the crossing of the Levada do Caldeirão Verde at **Pico das**

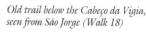

Old trail below the Cabeço da Vigia, seen from São Jorge (Walk 18)

Pedras (▲ ✕). Walk 21 and Short walk 21 both begin here. Some 250m further uphill you come to the Pico das Pedras forestry house (❀ ☴ with fireplaces). Beyond two well-sited viewpoints (☷ ☴), the first involving a climb, the road ends on a plateau. This is the **Achada do Teixeira** (79km ☷ ☴), where Walk 19 ends and Walk 20 begins. You could picnic here (*P*20) at Homem em Pé (photograph page 93) or on the Ruivo path (☴). Or you might like to walk to Queimadas* (☴ ❀ *P*22); if so, park down at Pico das Pedras.

Turn back to **Santana★** (93km *i* ♟ ☖ *P*26 and theme park of island culture), where Walk 18 begins and Walk 22 ends. Circular Walk 26 is a tour around Santana, taking in some of the best views. Break for lunch here, if you didn't bring a picnic. Then decide whether to press on to São Jorge (☖ ☷) or Arco (☷ ☴), returning the same way. You want to leave Santana at about 15.00.

Retrace your route to Faial. It's now afternoon, and you are just in time to enjoy the best views from the two *miradouros* (☷) west of the village or, lower down, the Fortim do Faial off to the left (take the first right off the signposted road). Clouds scud across the sky, creating fascinating mosaics of light and shade on this dramatic landscape. Eagle Rock is seen from base to summit, standing guard over church and village, at the confluence of three great river valleys: the Metade, the Seca and the São Roque. This superb panorama is likely to be one of your most lasting impressions of Madeira.

Beyond **Faial** turn right on the ER103 (✕). Look left to see São Roque atop its *lombo* (the spine separating the parallel ravines of the São Roque and Metade rivers), as you follow

---

*1.3km west of the ER218, a steep road climbs to Queimadas (Walks 22, 23, 28). Near the top, it is very narrow, with few passing places. It's usually easier to walk from Pico das Pedras (30 minutes each way).

28

Two walks from Boaventura:
the Levada de Cima (Walk 27a)
and Arco de São Jorge's
sugarloaf cliff (Walk 27b)

the road up the spectacularly terraced Seca Valley towards the mountains shown in silhouette on pages 84-85. Walk 21 ends at **Cruzinhas** (105km), in a magnificent splurge of cultivation (photograph page 96).

Just after you cross the Metade, pass a rough road right to the power station at Fajã da Nogueira (Walk 24). Climb past the fruit trees of **Achada do Cedro Gordo** and forests of cedar, cypress, pine and eucalyptus (⋒). Beyond a viewpoint (▨) left over the Ribeiro Frio Valley, you reach the sweet coolness of **Ribeiro Frio★** (111km ✗⋒❀●).

Take a break here to walk to Balcões (Short walk 25, page 104). From these 'Balconies' (▨*P25*) you have a view to contrast with that from the Juncal *miradouro* visited earlier in the day. Eagle Rock is seen again, presiding over the north coast villages. But from the Balcões the jagged central peaks dominate the scene. The Metade takes its source on these heights, and its tributaries feed the power station 250m/800ft below you (Walk 24), from where the Tornos Levada flows on to irrigate the southeast.

Beyond the trout hatcheries and small botanical garden, wind uphill (⋒) through conifers, back to **Poiso** (118km). Just 0.5km south of the pass, turn left on the ER203 signposted to 'Camacha'. Delicate Himalayan cedars grace the top end of this road, catching the sun. Ignore a turn-off left (to the dump!), but take the next turn-off right, to see the pretty **Montado do Pereiro** recreation area (△⋒), complete with bandstand. Return to the ER203 and continue down past some light industrial development (and lorries travelling up to the dump), to cross the Levada da Serra at Paradise Valley (Short walk 10-2). Half a kilometre further on, meet the ER205 and turn right, back to Funchal (143km).

Car tour 5: PORTO MONIZ AND THE PAÚL DA SERRA

Funchal • São Vicente • Seixal • Ribeira da Janela • Fanal
• Porto Moniz • (Achadas da Cruz) • Ribeira da Janela Valley
• Paúl da Serra • Bica da Cana • Encumeada • Funchal

*149km/92mi; 5 hours' driving, **excluding** the detour to the cable car at
Achadas da Cruz; take the Via Rápida west from Funchal.*

On route: ☔ at Vinháticos, Encumeada, Chão dos Louros, above
Rosário, Feiteiras, Porto Moniz, Fonte do Bispo, Rabaçal, Bica da Cana;
Picnics (see **P** symbol and pages 12-16): 31-33, 36, (37), 38, 39, (42);
Walks: 20, (29), 31-33, (35-37), 38, 39, (42). The 'Appetizer' walk
described on page 41 is also en route.

*This is the most beautiful tour to the west and combines especially well with Car
tour 4, to provide a two-day programme covering almost all of Madeira's best
landscapes. If you've already done Car tour 1, you could save some time by using
the Encumeada tunnel.*

Follow Car tour 1 to **São Vicente** (39km ✝⌂∩). North
of the village, turn left for Porto Moniz. The 'business-
men's route' along the north coast runs swiftly through
tunnels. (The spectacular old corniche route here, the 'Antiga
ER101', has unfortunately been chained off on account of
rockfall. It's hard to believe it was once the main road to Porto
Moniz — for two-way traffic, including coaches!).

Turn off right to **Seixal** (46km), where the church perches
high above the coast. Notice the steep vineyards here, edged
with feathery heath tree fencing. If you haven't brought a
picnic, Brisa Mar is a superb fish restaurant down by the sea
(follow 'Cais'). Not far past Seixal, a road signposted 'Praia'
leads to a pleasant seaside promenade and rock pools.

Continue on the coastal road west towards Ribeira da
Janela: village and river take their name from the 'window'
(*janela*) in the 'sea-horse' rock just off the coast. Just beyond
a tunnel and *before* a bridge and power station), turn off left
for 'Ribeira da Janela, Fanal'). Keeping right at a junction and
always climbing, you pass below the village church at **Ribeira
da Janela**. Some 12km uphill, turn left on a road signposted
'Posto Florestal do Fanal' (where a sign points ahead to the
Paúl da Serra). Keep left at a fork almost immediately, then
park just before a chained-off trail. The **Fanal★** forestry house
(65km △🏠) is just ahead to the right. Follow the old trail past
the forestry house and into a 'museum' of centuries-old *til*
trees (the laurels shown on page 8); stretch your legs on Walk
36 and picnic (**P**36).

Return the same way, enjoying a fine view back east along
the coast and down over the *janela* rock on the descent. Back
on the coastal road, turn left over the bridge, pass the power
station and go under the pipe carrying water from the reservoir
where Walk 42 begins. Soon you're in **Porto Moniz★** (79km
i△🏠🏠WC and 'living science' centre), where natural lava-rock
pools have been beautifully incorporated into an extensive

swimming complex with good facilities. The 'Appetizer' walk on page 41 ends here, having descended the sheer coastal cliffs behind the village.

Climb out of Porto Moniz on steep hairpin bends, past two bird's-eye viewpoints () over the village setting. Just 3.5km up from the roundabout by the petrol station, you pass the road off left to Walk 42 (*P*42), signposted to Lamaceiros. The 'Appetizer' walk mentioned above begins 100m before the church in **Santa**; it's a very steep, but technically easy descent to Porto Moniz. Beyond Santa the main tour turns left on the ER105 for Funchal at the cattle market (85km). (***Detour:*** First you could make a detour of 12km return to the cable car near Achadas da Cruz (): keep ahead to the signpost 'Miradouro, Teleférico', then turn right. Even if you don't take the hair-raising ride, the view straight down to Quebrada Nova, 640m/2100ft below, is breathtaking.)

The ER105 at first runs southeast, high above Madeira's greatest ravine. The far-off views over the north and south coasts are splendid. But even more impressive is the size and magnificence of the **Janela Valley**. Virgin forests of heath and laurel cloak the mountainsides like green sable.

Our first stop is at the ruined 'Casa do Elias' at **Quebradas** (90km), from where there is a superb view over Ribeira da Janela on its conical hilltop. Soon come to another *miradouro* near **Fonte do Bispo** (96km), from where the ER210 runs south down to Prazeres. If you have binoculars, looking southeast you can see the Rabaçal houses at the head of the valley … and even the Risco waterfall. Across the valley you can see the old laurels on the Fanal hillsides. Beyond the Fanal, the peaks in the east rise above cloud necklaces. The lighthouse at Ponta do Pargo is glimpsed in the west.

Paúl da Serra

At 103km, you pass the ER211 south to Calheta. The much-loved beauty spot, Rabaçal (⚏*P*37a-e; Walk 37) is most easily reached on foot from a barbecue building 2km down this cobbled road, *but you need a torch* (see page 128). Soon you reach the head of the valley, by a reservoir and parking area (⚏*P*38 and Walk 38; photograph page 131). Rabaçal lies 2km (200m/650ft) below; the road is closed to traffic, but a shuttle bus plies the route (see page 128). It's an easy walk down, but the re-ascent can be tiring.

Past the Pico da Urze (⚏⚏) you are on the **Paúl da Serra★**, so very different from the Janela Valley. Even in winter rain the Paúl has a strange beauty: the moors take on a golden hue, the bracken throws up wine-red flames, and seagulls swirl over the marshes. On sunny days, the air is bright as diamonds. Beyond the signpost left 'Fanal/Ribeira da Janela', you come to the ER209 south: both versions of Walk 35 begin 4km down this road. (Unfortunately, neither can be recommended for the duration of this edition: the fires of August 2016 ravaged these hillsides above Calheta.) Turn left for Bica da Cana, passing a statue to Nossa Senhora da Serra on the right. Walk 39 (photographs page 132) begins at the signpost left to 'Estanquinhos' (*P*39). But keep *right* here for **Bica da Cana**: two concrete pillars mark the stone-laid trail to this old hunting lodge, on your left (111.5km ⚏ and ⚏ at the end of the track above the house; *P*33 and Walk 33).

Continue on the ER105 for the breathtaking descent to Encumeada. You look out to the high peaks in the east, the landscape shown on page 119. Some 4.5km from Bica, a signpost on the right, 'Lombo do Mouro', alerts you to the refuge shown on page 116 (*P*31 and Walk 31). Just over 1km further on, Alternative walk 33 begins its climb to Pináculo opposite a sign for the PR17. Soon you skirt above the magnificent Rabaças and Norte levadas and follow them to **Encumeada★** (121km ⚏⚏✕). From here retrace your outgoing route to Funchal (149km).

On the descent to Porto Moniz ('Appetizer' walk described on page 41)

Car tour 6: THE SUNNY SOUTHWEST COAST

Funchal • Ribeira Brava • Prazeres • Ponta do Pargo • Achadas da Cruz • Fajã da Ovelha • Paúl do Mar • Jardim do Mar • Calheta • Ponta do Sol • (Ribeira Brava) • Funchal

147km/91mi; 6 hours' driving; Exit D from Funchal (plan pages 10-11)

On route: ⌂ at Campanário, Ponta do Sol, Arco da Calheta, Prazeres, east of Raposeira; Picnics (see *P* symbol and pages 12-16): (6, 34, 40); Walks (5), 6, 30, 31, 34, 35, 40, 41

This tour follows inland roads all the way west — for the views and the walks. We then return by the shorter coastal road and the expressway.

Leave Funchal by Exit D, passing the heavily built-up hotel area along the coast. Beyond Câmara de Lobos (Car tour 3), the ER229 winds below **Estreito de Câmara de Lobos** (Walk 6) and **Garachico**. Just 0.8km past the left turn to **Cabo Girão★** the road crosses the Levada do Norte at **Quinta Grande** (Short walk 6-2).* And 0.5km past the petrol station at the end of **Campanário** (🚍⌂) a road on the right signposted to 'São Paulo, Boa Morte' (among others) leads to Boa Morte (*P6*) and Fontes (Walk 5). Soon you're circling steeply down into **Ribeira Brava★** (31km *i*🏛M and ✝ founded in the 1500s), where Walks 30 and 31 end. There's a large covered car park on the west side of the river, by the sea.

Leaving, take the road just north of the car park (shown in the photograph on page 116), to climb the ER222 towards 'Canhas'. After about 8km Lombada da Ponta do Sol (✝) is signposted up to the right; a detour to the village would take you to the beautiful old manor *(solar)* visited on Walk 30. Just beyond the church in **Canhas** (43km) notice the first of the 14 Stations of the Cross on your right; after the last, on a straight stretch of road (🚍), there is a monument to St Theresa (✝). (Nearby is the taxi rank, if you are dropping off passengers for Walks 35-37). Not far along, the ER209 heads up right to the Paúl da Serra. Soon you come to two dramatic viewpoints (📷⌂) down over Madalena do Mar, 450m/1500ft below.

At **Arco da Calheta** you pass a road up right to Pico do Arco (📷✕), where there is another splendid viewpoint over Madalena do Mar. Walk 35a ends on the western outskirts of Arco, at **Loreto**. The Manueline church here (✝) demands a visit, if you are lucky enough to catch the key-holder on site.

Climb under mimosa to **Prazeres** (67km ⌂), where Walk 40 begins. A detour left to the hotel would take you to a splendid viewpoint over Paúl do Mar, 600m/2000ft below (📷 *P*40; photograph page 15). Walk 41, along the photogenic

---

*300m further on you could turn left to Junction 3 on the Via Rápida for an amazing experience: drive down under the motorway following the brown sign, 'Fajã dos Padres'. A 'lift' with windows will drop you almost 300m/1000ft straight down the cliffs west of Cabo Girão — to an idyllic stony beach and plantation (✕). You'll want to linger, so save this 4km detour for another day. This landslip is only accessible by lift or boat.

'Esmeraldo's domain', near Lombada da Ponta do Sol (Walk 30)

levada shown on page 135, starts just below the church at **Raposeira**. Pass the turn-off left to Faja da Ovelha (72km 🍴) and keep ahead to **Ponta do Pargo** (81km; Walk 34). Follow 'Farol'; this road (🔺) takes you to the lighthouse ★ (83km 📷), the island's most westerly point. A golf course is planned for this area, but funds have dried up. Head back 1km and turn right to the 'Miradouro', a viewpoint with a lovely tea house/restaurant (📷✗); from there you can drive back up to Ponta do Pargo's church and the main road.

Now turn right* and retrace your route east for 9km, then turn right on the ER223 (🍴) to **Faja da Ovelha**. Continue south (📷) to seaside **Paúl do Mar** (104km), where Walk 40 ends. Passing to the left of the church, bear left for Jardim do Mar, going into a tunnel. At the end of the tunnel, turn right into beautifully restored **Jardim do Mar**, where you can wander the pretty cobbled paths.

Leaving Jardim do Mar, return to the tunnel exit and turn right for 'Calheta'. Go through a short tunnel and, at the next junction, turn right for 'Funchal, Calheta'. Just 1km further on, keep straight ahead into a tunnel. Beyond an adjacent tunnel, at a roundabout, take the second exit for 'Calheta'. Entering **Calheta** (⚓🍴📷), you descend past the church on the right. Coming onto the seafront promenade, there is a pretty viewpoint on the right and the restored remains of an old *aguardente* (sugar cane spirit) factory a short way along to the left. But Calheta's main attraction is its marina and lido, with bijou sandy beaches either end. Keep ahead along the coast and, at the next roundabout, follow 'Funchal'.

Drive through the long, drab village of **Madalena do Mar** and, at the roundabout where Ponta do Sol is signposted left, keep straight ahead along the coast. You will pass some restored cottages on the left — the most attractive feature of Madalena (note the poignant shrine in the wall). More tunnels now carry you to **Ponta do Sol** (123km 🍴🍴 and ⚓ founded in the 15th century), where attractive façades grace another seaside promenade. Curve left uphill out of the village and, at a fork, *keep ahead* for 'Funchal'. At the roundabout, take the first exit, immediately going through another tunnel. **Lugar de Baixo** is reputed to be the sunniest place on Madeira. Following signs for Funchal, you can bypass Ribeira Brava and pick up the Via Rápida back to Funchal (147km).

*Or first detour left to the Boa Morte chapel (**P**34; see map page 120).

❀ Walking

Over 100 long and short walks are described in this Thirteenth edition, but you can devise many more for yourself. The majority of our walks are linear because they follow old trails and the levadas. If you have hired a car, don't be discouraged by the lack of circular walks. You can use your car and the buses (or taxis) in tandem. Suitable walks (not necessarily circular) are indicated by a 🚌 symbol in the Contents. It may be one of the *variations* of the main walk that is recommended: look for the 🚌 symbol under 'How to get there' (with waypoints for the walk start so that you can set your satnav).

Grading, waymarking, maps, GPS

We've tried to give you a quick overview of each walk's **grade** in the Contents. But many of our walks are very long, so we've split then up into as many as five sections — and even these may have shorter and alternative versions! In the Contents we've only had space to show the **lowest** grade of a *main* or *multi-section* walk *in fine, dry weather:* for full details, see the walk itself. Here is a brief overview of the four gradings:

- very easy — more or less level (perhaps with a short climb to a viewpoint); good surfaces underfoot; easily followed
- easy-moderate — ascents/descents of no more than about 300-500m/1000-1800ft; good surfaces underfoot; easily followed
- moderate-strenuous — ascents/descents may be over 500m/1800ft; variable surfaces underfoot — you must be sure-footed and agile; possible route-finding problems in poor visibility
- expert — only suitable for very experienced hillwalkers with a head for heights; hazards may include landslides or balancing on the narrow edges of levadas with no respite from constant exposure

Any of the above grades may, if applicable, be followed by:

⁞ *possibility* of vertigo — for those with no head for heights at all
⁞⁞ *danger* of vertigo — you must have a very good head for heights

Assigning grades to walks is *very* subjective — and giving them a 'vertigo' rating even more so! Until you get used to Madeira's terrain and know your 'vertigo tolerance', why not try walking with one of the many guided groups?

In common with the Canary and Balearic Islands, Madeira had EU support for repairing, **signposting** and **waymarking** many walking routes. The aim (not yet realised, due to financial constraints) was to number and waymark *all* island walks with standard European red and yellow flashes (two horizontal stripes mean *continue this way;* right- or left-angled stripes indicate a *change of direction;* X means *do not go this way*). Our text and maps include these waymarked routes (all

35

prefaced with 'PR') *where they existed at press date*. Once in a while you may find a path closed for maintenance; **information about path closures along the 'official', numbered government 'PR' routes is posted at www.visitmadeira.pt** (click on 'Walks' to see if there are any problems/closures).

Our walking **maps** were originally based on old 1:25,000 and 1:50,000 maps of the island published by the Portuguese government. Over the years we have updated these through our own research on foot or by car (using GPS readings) and printed them at a scale of 1:40,000. But the only paths shown on our maps are those we know to be viable *at time of writing*, even if they not described in the book. (For example, we include the footpaths in the Serra das Funduras near Portela, the path from Boca dos Namorados to Curral, and various 'PR' routes shown on the above-mentioned website.)

Note that some of the paths we show are very difficult or vertiginous; unless you are an expert, please stick to the walks described (those highlighted in green or violet).

Free **GPS track** downloads and **height profiles** are available for all our walks: see the Madeira page on the Sunflower website. Please bear in mind, however, that GPS readings — especially those taken in Madeira's many ravines — should *never* be relied upon as your sole reference point. Conditions can change at any time — especially on Madeira, where whole mountainsides come down overnight. GPS is hardly needed on Madeira anyway, but what *is* great fun is dragging our GPX files over Google Earth to preview the walks in advance!

Where to stay

If you have only a week on the island, or if walking is not your top priority, it's best to stay in **Funchal**. The bus network radiates from the capital. But the good news for keen walkers is that there are now *many hotels and apartments all over the island — in villages and in the mountains*, more frequent bus services, and more fly-drive packages than ever before. Judicious use of the bus timetables — together with a hired car, if you so choose — will take you to a good selection of walks *wherever* you are based. Ask your nearest Portuguese Tourist Office for the Madeira accommodation guide, or check the web: www.visitmadeira.pt.

Our walks pass by several 'rest houses' in Madeira's mountains. These are for the use of government officials, school parties, etc — not for foreign visitors (although you will be welcome to picnic in the grounds).

Just recently, Madeira has taken to **camping** in a big way, with many campsites: see www.madeira-camping.com; there are also a few **youth hostels**: see www.juventude.gov.pt/Portal/Lazer/en and click on 'Choose a region'.

Weather

Madeira has fine walking weather all year round, although summer is most reliable (and usually not too hot). Equinoctial rains can be expected in spring and autumn, but there will be many fine days as well. We tend to avoid June and early July, however, as the island is often covered by a 'hood' of low-lying clouds (the *capacete*).

Safe walking demands accurate reading of the weather signs and common sense. Outside summer many walks, especially in the north and west, can be treacherous. Even on the most glorious winter's day, levada paths will be full to overflowing and some mountain trails like waterfalls. *Never forget that anywhere on the island, at any time of year, a landslide can wipe out a path overnight.*

Apart from the seasons, Madeira's weather is determined by **wind direction**. Whatever the season, the weather will be at its best with a light northeasterly (trade) wind. If the wind swings round to west or (worst of all) southwest, unsettled weather follows. The central mountains catch up the clouds carried by these winds; read the signs to find the best 'microweather' for your walk:

- **Strong winds** from any direction except east, bring rain, if not storms. (Eg, if a strong northeasterly blows in, we head for the southwest.)
- **Strong wind from the east or south of east** *(leste):* This hot, dry wind from Africa should make for good walking everywhere.
- **Mild winds from any direction except south or south-west** afford good walking all round the island, although the northern valleys may be cloudy.
- **Mild winds from the south/southwest** bring rain!
- As a rule of thumb, the **Desertas Islands** can serve as a 'ready-reckoner' for weather signs:
— If they are clearly visible (wind from W of N): the southeast, northeast and east are clear — at least in the valleys. The west is cloudy.
— If they are hazy or hardly visible (wind from the E, S, SE): the south may be cloudy, but walking is generally good everywhere.
— If they are cloudy (wind from the NE): the west, southwest and northwest are clear; eastern areas may be cloudy.
— If they seem very close and there is a white line on the horizon (wind from S, SW): rain is coming within 24 hours.
- The old adage invariably holds true: 'red sky at night, walkers' delight; red sky in the morning, take warning!'
- Telephone 12 150 for a recorded weather forecast *in Portuguese*, or see the local newspapers.
- The general pattern is a clear morning, with clouds gathering by mid-day, and the sky clearing again by mid-afternoon. *Early starts are recommended!*

What to take

If you are already on Madeira and haven't walking boots or a torch or rucksack, you can still do many of our walks. But don't attempt the more difficult ones without proper equipment. For each walk in this book, we tell you the *minimum* equipment necessary. Where we require walking boots, there is *no substitute:* you will need to rely on the grip and ankle support they provide, as well as their waterproof qualities. For all other walks wear stout lace-up shoes with thick rubber or 'Vibram'-type soles, to provide good grip. Do *not* venture on walks requiring a torch unless you have one — some levada tunnels are exceedingly long, and you *must* be able to see both the roof (for possible projections) and the path, because the water in the channel may be very deep, cold, and fast-moving.

You may find the checklist below useful:

walking boots
extra pair of socks and bootlaces
waterproofs (outside summer)
long-sleeved shirt (sun protection)
long trousers, tight at the ankles
fleece
bus timetables (see page 9)
telescopic walking pole(s)
'Dog Dazer' (see 'Nuisances')
sunhat, suncream, sunglasses

mobile (the **pan-European emergency number is 112**)
torch (with a wide beam)
whistle, compass
first-aid kit; bandages
plastic groundsheet
water flask; water purifying tablets
plates, cups, knives, openers
water shoes (for swimming from stony beaches)

Please bear in mind that we've not done *every* walk in this book under *all* weather conditions: we may not realise just how hot — or wet — some walks might be. Walking boots are *always* more useful than shoes, and we wear them all year round. In hot weather, *always* carry a long-sleeved shirt as well as your sunhat, and take your lunch in a shady spot. We rely on your good judgement to modify our equipment lists according to the season.

Nuisances

Dogs are not often a problem, but a 'Dog Dazer' (an ultrasonic dog deterrent) is a good investment; Dazers are available on the web. There are *no* snakes, scorpions, poisonous spiders, or any other 'nasties' on the island.

Large **groups of walkers**, whether travelling by coach or in fleets of mini-buses or 4WDs, may cause your heart to sink, and they seem to invariably stop for lunch at the places recommended in this book. If you know they are on your path, it may be best to stop somewhere else to picnic.

Robberies have been a sporadic problem over the years on the very popular levadas near low-income housing (Walks 1, 6, 7). Although we've not heard of anyone being attacked,

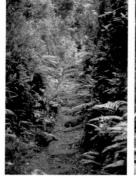

Wait till your knees are used to Madeira's terrain before tackling steep descents like the path to Ilha (left, Walk 28) or the steps down the Levada do Bom Sucesso (right, Walk 8)

the youths (unemployed and after drug money) sometimes have knives. People walking alone or in couples are vulnerable, so keep in close range of other walkers. The police are aware of the problem and 'patrol' by posing as walkers.

Portuguese for walkers

Once you venture off the beaten track, few of the older people speak English (the young people often speak English, German or French). We have found an almost foolproof way to ask *and understand* directions in Portuguese. First, memorise the key questions and all their possible answers below; then **always phrase your questions so that you will get a yes ('seng') or no ('nowgn') answer.**

KEY QUESTIONS (English/approximate Portuguese pronunciation)

'Please, sir (madam).	**Fahz** fah-**vohr**, sehn-**yohr** (sehn-**yoh**-rah).
Where is the levada to ...	**Ohn**-deh eh al leh-**vah**-dah **pah**-rah ...
(the main road to ...,	(ah ish-**trah**-dah **pah**-rah ...,
the footpath to ...,	ah veh-**ray**-dah **pah**-rah ...,
the way to ...,	oh cah-**mee**-noo **pah**-rah ...,
the bus stop)?	ah **pah**-rah-**jeng**)?
Many thanks.'	**Mween**-too o-bree-**gah**-doo (a woman says: '**Mween**-too o-bree-**gah**-dah).

POSSIBLE ANSWERS (English/approximate Portuguese pronunciation)

here/there	ah-**key**/ah-**lie**
straight ahead/behind	**semp**-reh eng **frengt**/ah-**traash**
to the right/to the left	ah deh-**ray**-tah/ah ish-**kehr**-dah
above/below	eng **see**-mah/eng **bye**-joo

Ask a native speaker (your hotel porter, tour rep or taxi driver) to help you with the pronunciation of these key phrases, as well as *place names*.

When you have your mini-speech memorised, always ask the many questions you can concoct from it in such a way that a yes/no answer will result. *Never* ask an open-ended question such as 'Where is the main road?' Even if you are standing on it, you probably won't understand the answer! Instead, ask the question and then **suggest the most likely answer yourself**, for example:

'**Fahz** fah-**voor**, sehn-**yoo**-rah. **Ohn**-deh eh ah ish-**tra**-dah **pah**-rah Foonshal? Eh **sem**-preh eng **frengt**?' or '**Fahz** fa-**vohr**, sehn-**yor**. **Ohn**-deh eh ah Le-**vah**-dah dosh **Tor**-nosh? Eh eng **see**-mah ah deh-**ray**-tah?'

An inexpensive phrase book will help you compose other 'key' phrases and answers. It is always pleasant to greet people you meet on your walks with a 'good morning' or 'good afternoon' (bohm **dee**-ah, bo-ah **tard**).

Organisation of the walks
Our walks are grouped in three general areas: the southeast; the northeast and the great peaks; the west and northwest. We urge you to walk in *each* of these three areas, in order best to sample the island's varied landscapes.

We hope that the book is set out so that you can plan your walks easily — depending on how far you want to go, your abilities and equipment, the season ... and what time you are willing to get up in the morning!

You might begin by looking at the fold-out touring map inside the back cover. Here you can see at a glance the overall terrain, the extent of the levada network, main and secondary roads, and the orientation of the walking maps in the text. Flipping through the book, you'll see that there is at least one photograph for each walk.

Having selected one or two potential excursions from the map and the photographs, turn to the relevant walk. At the top of the page you will find planning information: distance/ time, grade, equipment, and how to get there. If the grade and equipment specifications are beyond your scope, don't despair! *We almost always suggest a short version of each walk* and, in most cases, these shorter walks are far less demanding of agility and equipment.

When you are on your walk, you will find that the text begins with an introduction to the overall landscape and then quickly turns to a detailed description of the route itself. Times are given for reaching certain key checkpoints. *Do compare your pace with ours on one or two short walks before tackling a long hike!* **Note that our times do not include any stops!** Allow extra time for picnics, photography, and any other breaks.

Below is a key to the **symbols** on the walking maps.

═══	expressway/main road	●▸	waterfall, tank, tap	✢✢	church.chapel
───	secondary road	P	picnic suggestion (see pages 12-16)	⊞	cemetery
───	minor or urban road	🖼	best views	†	shrine, statue
───	track	⁑	danger! vertigo!	⋔	picnic site with tables
----	footpath, cobbled trail	🚌	bus stop	⛩	map continuation
3→	main walk	🚗	car parking	⋏	wind farm
3→	alternative walk	■	specified building	⛏	power station
───	levada, pipe	] [	tunnel	⋀	radio/TV mast
2→	levada walk	—600—	altitude (metres)	☕	bar/shop, café
				❶ ❷	start/end, waypoint

Appetizer: FROM SANTA TO PORTO MONIZ

See photograph page 32   **Distance:** 3km/2mi; 1h15min

Grade: ● moderate; a steep descent of 450m/1475ft. You must be sure-footed, but there is no danger of vertigo. *Virtually no shade*

Equipment: stout shoes (walking boots preferable), sunhat, optional picnic, water, walking stick, bathing things

How to get there: 🚌 80 or 150 to Santa; or 🚗 (Car tour 5): park by the public WC, 100m northeast of the church (32° 51.594'N, 17° 11.418'W). *To return:* 🚌 80 from Porto Moniz, back to base, or back to your car at Santa (or 🚌 139 to Funchal, but this does not go via Santa)

While road-building has ruined many of Madeira's old trails, several relatively short stretches still remain and have even been restored. Walks 15, 18, 27b and 40, and Alternative walk 25-1 all include sections of old cobbled trails. This 'Appetizer' is the perfect way to stretch your legs on a car or bus tour to the northwest. The best way to do it is to drive or take a bus to Santa in the morning, walk slowly down, savouring the views, then have lunch and a swim at the sea-water pools in Porto Moniz, before catching the 4pm bus — back to base, or back to your car.

Start out on the main road in **Santa**, 100m northeast of the church: just before the walled-in CEMETERY, turn left down CAMINHO DA IRMÃ DO PERPETUO SOCORRO (○). Go straight over two crossroads and, when the tar ends, continue down a *very steep* concrete lane, already enjoying superb views over Porto Moniz and the large sea-water pool complex. When the concrete lane ends (**20min**), take concrete STEPS off right (❶): these quickly give way to the old zigzag trail — much easier on the knees. The trail eventually runs into a valley — a pleasant shady interlude, before descending near the ER101.

Ignore a minor road off to the right, and when you pass near the restaurant/viewpoint on the right (on the second hairpin bend), keep left downhill on another road. But after the hairpin bend to the right, watch for your turn-off left — on a narrower, steeper cobbled trail. Concrete steps take you down to a narrow LEVADA (❷) not far above the school in **Porto Moniz**. Follow it to the right, then descend by road and steps (with street lights) to the POOL COMPLEX (**1h15min**). The bus leaves from the ROUNDABOUT (○) just above the pools.

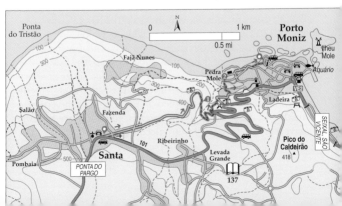

137

Walk 1: THE SOCORRIDOS VALLEY

Distance: 10.7km/6.6mi; 3h20min   **See also photograph page 7**

Notes: There is a noisy rock-crushing plant in the lower valley. Try to save the main walk for a Sunday (the Alternative walk is not affected). It is also possible to begin the walk at Barreiros Stadium (*town* 🚌 45; see plan pages 10-11), but the area surrounding the levada is very built-up.

Grade: ●❓ moderate, with an ascent of 150m/500ft to the Curral Levada. Very narrow footpaths: you must be sure-footed and agile. *Possibility of vertigo,* but railings protect most exposed sections. ***Important:*** The walk along the Levada do Curral is out-and-back; after the 2h15min-point it is potentially ***very dangerous;*** read the notes on page 44 carefully.

Equipment: stout shoes, sunhat, long-sleeved shirt, picnic, water

How to get there: *town* 🚌 3 to Quebradas mini-market. The stop is 400m west of the large satellite dish, so ring the bell when you pass the dish; the small supermarket is across the road from the bus stop.

To return: town 🚌 8 or 16 from Madeira Shopping

Alternative walk: Levada do Curral. ●❓ 7.5km/4.7mi; 2h. Grade/equipment as main walk (but no ascent). Access: *town* 🚌 8 or 16 or 🚗 car to Madeira Shopping (32° 39.552'N, 16° 57.080'W). Walk downhill past the 'Burger King' tower (**○**) on your left, and turn right immediately past the 'CEMA' building. After 100m/yds you can join the double-channelled Levada do Curral, which runs beside the road, on your right. (There are some narrow stretches here, as it rounds a tiny valley.) In 10min the narrow lane up from Pinheiro das Voltas comes in from the left, just before house 121 (**❸**). Now follow the main walk from the 1h28min-point to the end.

The magnificent Socorridos is the focal point for this walk. Just behind the noisy 'Ruhr Valley' river mouth, we are drawn into a magnificent tapestry of cultivation … which eventually unravels at a spectacular gorge.

Start at the BUS STOP opposite **Quebradas** MINI-MARKET (**○**). Continue west along the bus route for 200m/yds, to the school and then a tiled tap dated 1938 (both on your left). Opposite the tap, on the north side of the road, you join the **Levada dos Piornais** (covered with concrete slabs). As you begin to round a small valley, the Socorridos bridge can be seen ahead. In **35min** you come to an information panel about the Piornais Levada, opposite a road left to Lombada.

Now the levada turns north. The ground falls away, and you edge the breathtaking **Ribeira dos Socorridos**. Within the next 10 minutes, take a break to admire the 'winged' bridge and the valley's tapestry of terracing. Think back to the days when sugar cane grew thick in the wide river bed below, and you can easily imagine how nuns from the Santa Clara Convent fled to Curral under cover of cane in 1566.

Continuing along the levada, you will probably marvel at the golden curves of this watercourse hewn in the side of the rock … sheer sculpture. Now you approach a series of short TUNNELS (no torch needed). Although the path through them is well protected, some people will find this stretch vertiginous. If you *do* go through the tunnels, ***you will have to stoop down very low, so take off your rucksack, or it will catch on the***

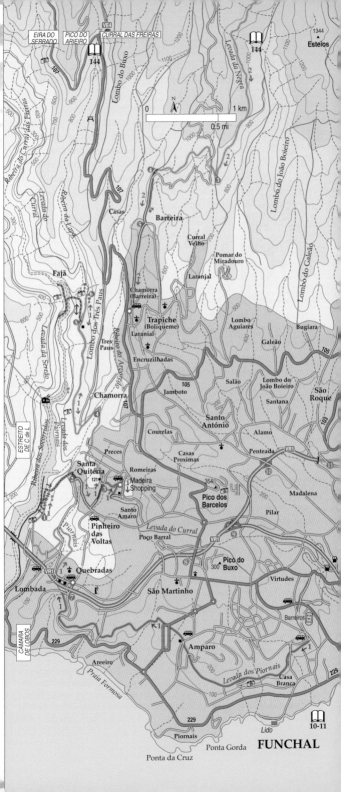

EIRA DO SERRADO
PICO DO ARIEIRO **144**
CURRAL DAS FREIRAS
Esteios

144

Ribeira do Curral das Freiras
Levada do Curral
Ribeira do Lapa
Levada da Serrão
ESTREITO DE C de L
Ribeira dos Socorridos
Levada das Piornais

Lombo do Buxo

Levada da Negra

Lombo do João Boieiro

Lombo do Galeão

Casas

Barreira

Curral Velho

Pomar do Miradouro

Laranjal

Lombo dos Três Paus

Ribeira do Arvoedo

Chamorra (Barreira)

Trapiche (Boliqueme)

Laranial

Laranjal

Encruzilhadas

Três Paus

Lombo Aguiares

Galeão

Bugiara

Chamorra

Jamboto

Salão

Lombo do João Boieiro

São Roque

105

Santo António

Courelas

Alamo

Santana

103

Preces

Casas Proximas

Penteada

Santa Quitéria

Romeiras

Madeira Shopping

354

Madalena

Santo Amaro

Pico dos Barcelos

Pilar

Pinheiro das Voltas

Levada do Curral

Poço Barral

VR1

Quebradas

300

Pico do Buxo

Virtudes

Lombada

São Martinho

Barreiros

CÂMARA DE LOBOS

229

Areeiro

Amparo

Levada dos Piornais

Casa Branca

229

Praia Formosa

100

229

Piornais

Lido

10-11

Ponta Gorda

Ponta da Cruz

FUNCHAL

Levada do Curral near the isolated house (2h15min)

roof. Otherwise, just follow the arrow and descend steps to a PATH which runs below the tunnels (**1**).

Whichever route you choose, you will come to crossing concrete steps, where you turn right uphill. When the steps stop (10 minutes above the levada, by a house and a sign 'Vereda do Pico da Lombada' on the left), turn right on a CONCRETE WALKWAY (**2**) with street lights. Join a road at a T-junction and continue left uphill. In under 15 minutes from the top of the steps (**1h20min**) you reach a junction at **Pinheiro das Voltas**. Turn *left* here, climbing a lane, the TRAVESSA DO PINHEIRO DAS VOLTAS. The lane narrows. In eight minutes you reach the **Levada do Curral** at a T-junction with a road (**3**). Turn left here, passing house No 121 on the left.

Now follow the levada past some pretty houses and gardens. After a brief diversion into the shady head of the **Ribeira do Arvoredo** (**4**), you soon find yourself once again at the edge of the Socorridos.

When the houses end (**1h55min**), continue ahead; railings provide psychological comfort, and the route is not dangerous at this point. In under **2h15min** some well-tended vines spring up by a pretty, ISOLATED HOUSE. Ignore a path down to the left through the vegetable plots 80 paces beyond it (**5**).* About 400m/yds past the house you will pass through a GATEWAY (perhaps without even noticing), beyond which the way becomes *very dangerous. Go only as far as you feel comfortable.* The path approaches a sheer escarpment — the awesome, jungle-like gorge of the **Ribeira da Lapa** (**6**). Ahead of you the aptly named hamlet of Fajã ('landslip') sits abandoned on a hillside. Below you the Ribeira da Lapa joins the Ribeira do Curral and the two become the Socorridos. When you consider that these rivers cut the valley and today feed four *major* levadas, you can perhaps imagine what a torrent the Socorridos was when some of Zarco's men very nearly drowned in it (the word *socorridos* means 'rescued men').

Now turn back and *keep on the levada* past house 121, then make your way to MADEIRA SHOPPING (**3h20min**) — far nicer than its 'Burger King' tower would suggest! The BUS SHELTER (**O**) shown on our map is where buses 8 and 16 stop.

*Experienced walkers could take this *very steep and slippery* path down to the confluence of the Lapa and Curral (allow 45min return and keep left at a fork partway down). Once down in the chasm, the source of the lower levada on the western side of the Socorridos lies not far to the left; the source of the Levada dos Piornais is just north of the Ribeira da Lapa.

Walk 2: FROM THE POÇO DA NEVE TO BARREIRA

Map begins on the reverse of the touring map and ends on page 43; photographs pages 6, 13 and 39 (right)

Distance: 8.7km/5.4mi; 2h40min

Grade: ● ‼ fairly strenuous; a steep descent of 900m/2350ft. You must be sure-footed and have a head for heights (***danger of vertigo***).

Equipment: walking boots, walking stick(s), sunhat, picnic, water; fleece, long trousers and windproof in cool weather

How to get there: 🚕 *taxi* to the Poço da Neve (ice house) on the ER202 2km below Pico do Arieiro, or 🚌 103 or 138 to Poiso (add 5km/3mi and 270m/885ft of ascent; 1h30min). The ice house is *below* the road, behind a walled lay-by.
To return: town 🚌 10A from Barreira (part of Chamorra)

Shorter walk: Poço da Neve — sheep pens viewpoint — Poço da Neve. ● 4.6km/2.8mi; 1h20min. Moderate; no danger of vertigo. Stout shoes, sunhat. Access: 🚕 car or *taxi* to/from the Poço da Neve (32° 43.558'N, 16° 55.485'W). Follow the main walk for 35min, then return the same way.

Alternative walk: Short walk 19 — Poço da Neve — Barreira. ● ‼ 11km/6.8mi; 4h45min. 🚕 *taxi* to Pico do Arieiro. Very strenuous; equipment, return as main walk. Follow Short walk 19 (page 89) to the second viewpoint, then return and walk down to the ice house to start this walk.

Note: Violet lines on our map indicate waymarked paths (yellow/red stripes) linking Arieiro, the Ribeira de Santa Luzia and the ice house. Use them to start the main walk or avoid the ER202 on the Alternative. At Arieiro, the path starts just behind the walkers' sign and skirts a dyke initially; the fork to the Ribeira de Santa Luzia may be overgrown at first.

A thoroughly exhilarating walk: glistening moorlands, a ribboning levada, and tremendous views. But wait till you've acquired your 'Madeira knees' — it's steep! So steep that it's unlikely any of the ice had a chance to melt back in the early 1900s, when men shouldering the precious commodity (wrapped in straw and packed in leather bags) fairly *ran* from the *poços da neve* ('snow pits') below Arieiro down to Funchal. The ice was not just served up in sorbets and drinks to the sybarites, it had important medical uses — to staunch bleeding, for example. Today only one ice house has been preserved, from where two paths plunge down to Funchal: one runs down the Santa Luzia Valley and the other, our path, down the more westerly Santo António Valley.

Start out at the domed ICE HOUSE (**O**; *P2*) high on the eastern flanks of the **Ribeira de Santa Luzia**. Your route begins on the *western* side of the valley, where you can see a road on the ridge. It's a continuation of the road 250m/yds below the ice house shown in the photograph on page 13. So just take one of the paths down to it — *ignoring* a crossing path (perhaps with red/yellow waymarking posts) some 35m/yds downhill as well as any signposts for 'Levada do Barreiro'. (The Barreiro route follows a levada on the *eastern* side of the Santa Luzia Valley down to the Parque Ecológico Information Centre mentioned in the footnote on page 26. When we

45

did this walk many years ago it was horrendous. It was repaired and is now the official PR4, but was dreadfully damaged in the fires of 2010 and is still closed as this edition goes to press.

Turn right on the road and follow it across the valley. (The concrete walls in the river bed help to control flash flooding.) The road rises to a cattle grid where it meets the very narrow **Levada da Negra** (❶; **25min**). Ignoring the track on the left, turn left on the levada and follow it down a new valley — the **Ribeira de Santo António**. The path is quite overgrown or eroded in places, and some people will find it vertiginous; be prepared for a few scrambles on all fours. The city reveals itself in the V of the river valley. A rocky moonscape, with gnarled white heath tree limbs, alternates with ferny glens. (The long barren stretches of this route will be replanted; work had already begun before the disastrous mudslides and fires of 2010.) Where the grassy pastureland is broken, luscious gold and russet volcanic hues emanate from the rock. On rounding a bend (**35min**), a picturesque spread of circular rock-built SHEEP PENS (❷) appears on the right, stretching along a small plateau — the setting for an annual shearing festival on 10th June. *(The Shorter walk heads back here.)*

At **55min** you cross to the western side of the river. Fed by some new streams, the levada is now slightly wider. A few minutes after crossing the river you have to climb above the levada, to avoid a gully with a pipe. A few more awkward gullies follow; again you'll have to be nimble. By **1h35min**, after you have passed below the trig point marking the summit of **Esteios**, there is a superb view down to the twin spires of Santo António's church; the single slender spire of São Martinho is silhouetted against the sea. Looking back up the valley, you can trace your route almost back to the sheep pens.

In just **1h45min** you pass through a gate and the steep descent ends, as you contour beneath a canopy of dense eucalyptus trees. In **1h50min**, two levadas shoot down to the left by a tiny WATERHOUSE (❸). Cross them and keep straight on, along this narrow and sometimes slippery red clay path. Two minutes later you cross a road. In **2h10min** you begin a new descent: turn left down a COBBLED TRAIL (❹), with a rushing levada on your left. Enjoy another superb view — stretching from Boa Nova in the east to Cabo Girão in the west. After 100m/yds, pick up a road and follow it to the right.

At a Y-fork with a car park to the right (❺; **2h 20min**), ignore the tarred road to the left; keep straight downhill *past* the stop for bus 90/91 (which only operates in the north of the city) to reach the **Barreira** STOP for bus 10A (❻; **2h40min**).

Walk 3: FROM THE EIRA DO SERRADO TO CURRAL

Map on reverse of the touring map

Distance: 3.4km/2mi; 1h30min

Grade: ● moderate descent of 450m/1475ft. In autumn and winter fallen chestnut leaves obscure the path, so watch your footing. The descent can be slippery underfoot and hard on the knees.

Equipment: stout shoes or walking boots, sunhat, water, optional picnic

How to get there: 🚗 (Car tour 3) to the Eira do Serrado (32° 42.612'N, 16° 57.750'W) or 🚌 81 (*check in advance: not all 81 buses call at the Eira!*)
To return: 🚌 81 — frequent departures to Funchal, but few back to the Eira, if you left a car there (Mon-Fri 14.30, 16.15; Sat 14.30; Sun 13.00)

Until the 1950s the post (with vital funds sent home by emigrants) was carried from Funchal to Curral by a woman. Climbing and descending via the Eira, with her precious deliveries balanced in a basket on her head, she counted 52 hairpin bends each way. We follow the easiest part of her daily round.

Start out at the **Eira do Serrado** (○). First climb the aloe-fringed path at the left of the beautifully situated hotel; it leads to the famous VIEWPOINT (①). Then return and descend the steps at the right of the sign 'EIRA DO SERRADO ALT. 1094 m' (**15min**). The steps lead into a beautiful old cobbled trail below chestnut trees. You clear the trees five minutes down, to be greeted by superb views (*P3*) — and you won't have to share them.

As the trail makes a V-turn to the left, you are just level with the entrance to the old road tunnel under the Eira ('Antiga 107', chained off on account of rockfall — like the 'Antiga 101' on the north coast west of São Vicente). On the far side of the Ribeira do Curral, the houses of Casas Próximas teeter on the *lombo* plunging off Pico do Serradinho.

View to Curral das Freiras, near the end of the descent

S-bends take you past a couple of well-placed promontories; one of them (with an electricity pylon; **45min**) is a particularly pleasant picnic spot. From here there is a view back left to the first part of Walk 4: trees mark the Boca da Corrida, and the 'dip' between Pico Grande (with the twin summits) and Pico do Serradinho (to the left) is the Boca do Cerro saddle.

Then the sometimes-narrow path continues to drop sharply in more S-bends. In summer the surrounding cliffs are bright with yellow-flowering houseleeks. Soon you're just opposite Curral's church, in the setting shown on the previous page, and eventually concrete steps take you down to the ROAD (**1h15min**).

You could turn left downhill to the nearest BUS STOP (5min), but we suggested that you walk 800m uphill into **Curral** (**1h30min**) — and sample some unforgettable chestnut soup or cake! The bus leaves from the stop opposite the Sabores do Curral restaurant.

Walk 4: the massive escarpment of Pico Grande, seen ahead, will rise 300m/1000ft sheer above us beyond the Boca do Cerro.

Walk 4: BOCA DA CORRIDA • PICO GRANDE • ENCUMEADA

Map on reverse of the touring map; photograph opposite

Distance: 13km/8mi; 4h

Grade: ● ‼ moderate ups and downs, with an overall climb of about 300m/1000ft and descent of 500m/1650ft; you must be sure-footed. Below the escarpment of Pico Grande the well-built, paved path (PR12) is narrow (*possibility of vertigo*) and *may be closed for maintenance* if there has been a landslide or fire. It is in fact officially closed as we go to press.

Equipment: walking boots, long trousers, sunhat, picnic, plastic bottle/ water purifying tablets, whistle; extra fleece, windproof in cool weather

How to get there: 🚌 any of the many buses to Estreito de Câmara de Lobos; then *taxi* to Boca da Corrida. For those loath to spend the (fairly high) taxi fare: take 🚌 96 to 'Corrida' (08.05, 09.45) from where it is a *very steep 25min climb* to Boca da Corrida, where the walk begins. *To return:* 🚌 6 from Encumeada (*only one a day; don't miss it!*)

Alternative walks

1   Boca da Corrida — Boca do Cerro — Corrida or Corticeiras.
● 11.5km/7mi; 3h30min. Fairly easy. Stout shoes, sunhat, picnic, water. Access as for main walk; return on 🚌 96. Follow the main walk to Boca do Cerro; then return to Boca da Corrida and walk down the road from the forestry house. For the return buses, see the top paragraph on page 52 (at the 4h30min-point). Or 🚗 to/from Boca da Corrida (32° 42.660'N, 16° 59.207'W); this shortens the walk by 4.5km/1h10min.

2   Pico Grande summit and down to Curral: ● ‼ 8.7km/5.4mi; 4h30min. Ascent: 700m; descent : 1000m. See the footnote on page 50.

If we had to choose our favourite mountain walk on the island, it would probably be this one. There is so much to recommend it: not only are the views magnificent throughout, but there's very little climbing! But alas, over the years the route became one of the island's most popular walks, horribly eroded by large groups of walkers. The old grassy trail disappeared years ago, and today there is paving on some of the most heavily eroded and narrowest sections.

At the pass of **Boca da Corrida** there is a forestry house, a shrine, and a spectacular viewpoint over Curral das Freiras to the high peaks. As you face north, looking to the right of the shrine, Pico Grande rises ahead of you, framed in the V between Pico do Cavalo to the left and Pico do Serradinho to the right. Pico Grande is John's favourite mountain and easily identified from all over the island because of the rocky knoll on its summit. You'll see a path on the hillside to the left, but this is *not* our path. Out route is higher up and, for the moment, hidden from view.

Begin the walk by taking the stone-laid trail at the left of the SHRINE (**O**). In 30m/yds turn right (ignore the concreted track on the left between pillars; it is the Alternative walk 5 return from the remains of Montado dos Aviceiros). Follow the sign 'PR12, CAMINHO REAL DA ENCUMEADA, 12,6 KM', climbing a paved and stepped path. (The path to the right goes to another viewpoint.) After **8min** the walk levels out and, from a promontory on the right, there are fine views of the high mountains towering above Curral.

The Vinháticos *pousada* and the Paúl da Serra come into focus from the **Boca dos Corgos**, a pass reached in **30min**. (Be sure to ignore the old trail down sharp left to Serra de Água here; it is completely broken away.) Beyond the **Passo de Ares** (**45min**), the path describes a wide arc along the flanks of **Pico do Serradinho**. By **1h10min** you reach the fourth pass, the **Boca do Cerro** (**❶**). *(The Alternative walk turns back here.)* Beyond the Boca do Cerro, our route (which was the main north/south trail over the island in the 1800s) narrows appreciably, but it is easily discernible. Turn down left* through the prickly gorse and soon begin to skirt the awe-inspiring escarpment of **Pico Grande**. It will take 20-25 minutes to pass this rock face, and expect to get your feet wet! Then you hit paving again, following a 'Great Wall of China' down and round for over half an hour.

Beyond another escarpment, the **Fenda do Ferreiro**, you reach a sunny promontory above the knolls of **Piquinhos** (**2h05min**), where a short path off left leads to more fine views towards the Paúl da Serra (**❷**). About three minutes after the long paved section ends (**2h20min**), ignore a path down sharp left — if you even notice it.

Soon you near the head of the enchanting valley of the **Ribeira do Poço**, emerald green and dotted with the few *palheiros* of **Curral Jancão** on grassy abandoned terraces. The main river is crossed on a grass-covered STONE BRIDGE (**❸**; **2h45min**), with inviting rock pools below. A few lovely log bridges take you across further streams, and a promontory on the left overlooks the Pousada dos Vinháticos. If you spot it, ignore a path down left to Serra de Água (**3h25**).

Contouring through eucalyptus woods (often fire-scarred), you pass under the PIPE (**❹**) carrying water from the Norte and Rabaças levadas (Walk 32; **3h45min**) down to the power station at Serra de Água. The path widens to a track, the Residencial Encumeada comes into view, and you meet the ER228 (**O**; **4h**). Wait for the BUS here: flag it down! Or walk 1km down to the *residencial* (10min), for a drink or snack.

*The path to the right quickly reaches Chão da Relva, a grassy area with chestnut trees, a lovely picnic spot. From here experienced hillwalkers can climb to the summit of Pico Grande (**❸**; **● ▮▮** 1h30min return) or descend to Fajã Escura, north of Curral (**❺**; **● ▮▮** 3h) or do both (4h 30min); both routes demand a head for heights and are dangerous when wet. The Pico Grande path forks left off the Fajã Escura path after a few metres; it is marked with cairns and intermittent paint spots. The two most exposed points (close to the bottom and again at the very top) are protected with frayed steel ropes — take care not to cut your hands! These routes are highlighted in violet.

Walk 5: FONTES • CHÃO DOS TERREIROS • TROMPICA • FONTES

Map on reverse of touring map; continuation pages 54-55

Distance: 11km/6.8mi; 3h35min

Grade: ● moderate climb and descent of 500m/1650ft on track. The initial ascent is tiring in hot weather.

Equipment: stout shoes (walking boots preferable), sunhat, picnic, water; extra fleece and windproof in cool weather

How to get there and return: 🚗 to Fontes (32° 42.124'N, 17° 1.239'W), above Boa Morte. Travelling on the ER229, the road is 0.5km west of Campanário and 5km east of Ribeira Brava; it is signposted 'São Paulo, Boa Morte' (among others). Travelling on the VR1, leave at Exit 2, drive uphill to the ER229 and follow signposting as above. The road runs through two tunnels (ignore signposting right to Lugar da Serra). At a roundabout at the end of the second tunnel, turn right and follow the sign for 'São Paulo', keeping to the left of the large industrial estate. Round the deep valley of the Ribeira Funda, ignore the turning left for Espigão, and drive past the impressive steps to São Paulo's church. Fontes is the next village, 1.4km north. Leave your car parked well off the road, so that the bus or any heavy lorry can turn round. Fontes is also accessible by 🚌 127 *from Ribeira Brava*.

Alternative walk: Fontes — Chão dos Terreiros — Trompica — Boca da Corrida — Corticeiras. 15.5km/9.6mi; 5h40min. ● ‡ Moderate, but you must be sure-footed on the narrow path in the Ribeira do Campanário. Equipment as above, but walking boots and long trousers recommended. Access by 🚌 127 or 🚗 *taxi*; return on 🚌 96 from Corticeiras. *This alternative is especially recommended for those travelling by bus. It used to be a much more attractive return route than the track used in the main walk, but the mudslides and fires of 2010 devastated the area. Although the ground cover has regenerated beautifully, the idyllic eco-hamlet of Aviceiros was completely destroyed.* Follow the main walk to the Trompica forestry house (🕓; 2h50min). Then climb up the earthen bank at the left of the track (passing through a gate almost immediately), to find a narrow path which circles the Ribeira do Campanário. If you come to any forks, be prepared to spend a little time searching out the correct path; remember not to lose height, as the path does rise very slightly. Some 20min from Trompica you'll be at the centre of the valley, with a knoll below you. Two river tributaries, with lovely rock pools, are crossed on stepping stones and, in 40min, you reach the remains of the lowest of the Aviceiros (ⓐ) houses. The area is quite green now, with wonderful fruit trees

Alternative walk: Aviceiros as we first saw it many years ago

— untouched. Climb straight ahead, passing what's left of the highest building, to meet a track. Turn right on this track for Boca da Corrida. You will walk through a desolate area where burnt trees penetrate the now-green underbrush of broom and ferns. Another track comes in from above you, on your left, in about 1h10min, and you reach the forestry house at Boca da Corrida 1h40min from Trompica (○; 4h30min). From here walk down the road from the forestry house. About 20 minutes down the road (1.6km), just past a bar, fork right to a BUS SHELTER (ⓑ) where you can catch a 96 'Corrida' bus (17.40 Mon-Fri, 17.05 Sat/Sun). Or, just 1km beyond the hotel at Jardim da Serra, at a junction sign-posted to 'Farmácia' and 'Hotel Qta do Jardim da Serra', you can catch a 96 'Foro' bus (ⓒ). Otherwise, turn left uphill for 450m/yds, to a bar opposite the pharmacy (ⓓ), where the 96 'Corticeiras' bus stops.

Here's a walk that shows you the great divide formed by the Ribeira Brava from an unusual perspective. Not only will you have fantastic views over the north/south cleft of this deep ravine, but the panorama encompasses all the high peaks (Walks 19 and 20), Pico Grande (Walk 4), and the entire eastern escarpment of the Paúl da Serra. What's more, this is one of the few island walks that we can whole-heartedly recommend as a varied and satisfying circuit for motorists.

At **Fontes** (○) the asphalt road to Lugar da Serra swings round to the right, but a very narrow tarred road rises at the right-hand side of Bar Fontes (at the left of the 'Fontes' sign). **Start out** by climbing this narrow road. It's a steep haul, especially tiring in hot weather (our timings take this into account), and there is *very little shade*. But *don't* be discouraged; once you reach the first pass, the way will become much more attractive and remain so for most of the walk.

The tar ends at the last houses, and a stony earthen track takes you futher up the right-hand side of the **Ribeira Grande**. Ignore all offshoots left and right. Within **35min** you will have crossed the **Ribeiro Frio** (❶) and be aiming for the first pass. On reaching it, look back to see the village of São Paulo.

From fields of thistles and broom you look back down to São Paulo — but this area was badly burnt in the fires of 2010.

Small herds of cows will be encountered throughout the walk, grazing freely on the slopes of the hills above you.

Within **50min**, at another pass, you begin to enjoy the best views on the walk — the Ribeira Brava basin comes into sight, as well as the Lombo do Mouro (Walk 31), Vinháticos, Pináculo (Walk 33), and Encumeada. As you round **Pico da Cruz (1h)**, be sure to keep right (south) on the track, where a path descends to the left. This area, shown in the photograph opposite, was burnt during the disastrous fires of 2010, but the regrowth is slowly gaining ground. In the past barley was grown up here (the reason for cutting the track), but it did not flourish. Yet another pass, reached in **1h10min**, opens up more views to the high peaks, from Grande round to Ruivo, via Pico do Gato and the Torres.

Beyond another pass (from where, if you look up half-left, you can spot the triangulation point on Chão dos Terreiros), you come to a Y-FORK (**❷**; **1h25min**). The track to the right is the return route but, for now, go straight ahead. After 50-100m/yds you may have to negotiate a GATE IN A FENCE. Some 15 minutes later (**1h40min**) you encounter ANOTHER FENCE WITH A MAKESHIFT STILE. In another seven minutes the track makes a 90° turn to the left and peters out at a pass (**1h50min**). Climb up half-right towards the summit — though you won't see the triangulation point from here. You will reach a fenced enclosure on the **Chão dos Terreiros** within seven minutes. There is a gap in the fence allowing access to the TRIAN-GULATION POINT (**❸**), but the views are just as good from outside the enclosure. From here you have a new outlook — over Curral's setting and even down to Funchal.

If you have time and the day is clear, it's worth spending some time up here to find your own favourite viewpoint! Then leave the triangulation point and retrace your steps to the fork first met in 1h25min (**2h25min**). Turn sharp left downhill. The track descends over a couple of CATTLE GRIDS and past minor tracks to the right and the left, which you ignore. By **2h45min** you're walking beneath sweet chestnuts and later eucalyptus. Five minutes later go over a third CATTLE GRID (**2h50min**). Concrete comes underfoot and, 150m/yds further on, you come to the **Trompica** FORESTRY HOUSE (**❹**), on your right. (*Here the Alternative walk leaves us, by taking the path up to the left of the track.*)

Continue down past the forestry house on the track. Allow 45 minutes for the tedious return to Fontes. Some 15 minutes below Trompica you pass a double WATER TANK on the right. One kilometre further on you come to a T-junction with an asphalt road. Turn right here (left goes to Lugar da Serra and Campanário), descending at first, then climbing gently back to **Fontes** (**❺**; **3h35min**).

Walk 6: LEVADA DO NORTE: FROM ESTREITO DE CÂMARA DE LOBOS TO BARREIRAS

Distance: 18.2km/11.3mi; 6h20min (but see Short walks below)

Grade: see Short walks

Equipment: stout shoes, sunhat, picnic, water, torch; extra fleece and windproof in cool weather

How to get there: 🚌 96 to the levada crossing, 0.7km north of Estreito's church; ask for the 'Levada do Norte' bus stop.
To return: 🚌 6, 7, 80, 127 or 148 from Barreiras

Short walks

1 Estreito — Nogueira (1h40min) or Cabo Girão (2h30min).
● ‼ Easy, but some narrow stretches demand a head for heights. Equipment/access as main walk. Follow the main walk for 1h35min and *flag down* a bus on the ER229. Or go on to Cabo Girão: continue on the levada but, instead of curling right through the tunnel at ❸, keep ahead alongside a narrow levada. Pass steps down left towards Câmara de Lobos and, 10 minutes later, turn right up *crossing* steps (❹), to a road. Follow this uphill through a garish tourist development to the viewpoint (ⓑ; 35min from the tunnel). If no 🚌 154 is due, catch a bus on the ER229.

2   Quinta Grande — Campanário. ● ⁝ 8km/5mi; 2h. Grade and equipment as main walk. Access: 🚌 6, 7, 123, 139, 142 or 148 to 'Ribeira da Quinta Grande', where the ER229 crosses the levada (**④**). Follow the main walk from the 2h10min-point to the 3h45min-point at **⑤**, then descend to the ER229 at Campanário (**ⓒ**; frequent buses).

3   Boa Morte circuit. 3.5km/2.2mi; 1h20min. ● Easy; *recommended for beginners or motorists*. Trainers suffice. Access/return: any 🚌 to Ribeira Brava, then 🚌 127 to Boa Morte (**ⓓ**). From Boa Morte follow the road signposted to São Paulo up to the levada and turn left; return to Boa Morte in time for 🚌 148. 🚗: Turn north off the ER229 0.5km west of Campanário for (among others) 'São Paulo, Boa Morte'. Drive through two tunnels, ignoring a right turn to Lugar da Serra. Turn left at the roundabout at the end of the second tunnel, cross the levada immediately, and park nearby (32° 40.806'N, 17° 2.394'W). By bus or car, follow the main walk from the 4h35min-point (**⑦**) to the 5h-point (**⑨**; *P6*) and return.

Alternative ending: ● ⁝⁝ **The 1500 steps.** *Sure-footed* walkers can end the main walk or Short walk 3 with a truly *spectacular* descent (walking stick recommended). Continue on the levada past the first lookout (5h), with more wonderful views over the valley. Ignore a path down left, cross

a stream and, 25 minutes along, cross over a path with street lights. Some 12 minutes later, turn left on a road down to Eira do Mourão (**C**). Then descend concrete steps from the upper end of the small parking bay on your left, following street lights. Almost 1500 steep steps will take you down 500m/1650ft to Fajã and the VE4, where you could catch 🚌 6 (to the right, opposite the stadium (**i**). Allow 1h30min for this descent (7h for the main walk; 2h35min for Short walk 3). But if you have missed the bus, you will have to walk another 2km south into Ribeira Brava.

All year round this is a superb walk through a landscape rich in cultivation, thanks to the waters of the Levada do Norte (see notes in Walk 32). Here in early autumn the grapes are harvested for some of Madeira's best-known wines; the valleys are thick with sugar cane and cherry trees.

When the bus roars up the hill at Estreito, you'll first pass the church and then a chapel on the left. Just round the next bend is the BUS STOP (**O**), called '**Levada (do Norte)**'. **The walk starts** here: continue left uphill towards 'Jardim da Serra', ignoring the road to Castelejo and Boca dos Namorados to the right. After just 20m/yds turn left on the signposted levada, below photogenic vine-bearing trellises. It's hidden under concrete here, but you'll hear it singing underfoot before long. When a road crosses the levada, follow it for about 100m/yds, then find the open levada on the right.

At about **20min**, just as you bend right into the narrow **Ribeira da Caixa**, two separate paths down left, a few minutes apart avoid awkward narrow ledges with overhanging rock. Soon you'll find yourself deep in the valley; in May it is smothered in cherry blossom. You cross a tributary and then the main river (**①**; **45min**) on levada bridges.

On leaving the valley, start counting churches to measure your progress. At **1h05min** here's the first, below at **Garachico** (see opposite). Five minutes later, take the *third* set of steps up to a road, where the levada is almost opposite (but if you want refreshment, take the *second* set of steps, to the signposted 'Bar' just uphill to the right, after which the levada is 25m/yds down the road). At **Nogueira**, the levada seems to end at a house (**②**; **1h35min**). Descend the concrete ramp/steps on the left and, when you meet a cobbled road, climb it to regain the levada. (*But end Short walk 1 by turning left on the road, down to the ER229.*)

In six to seven minutes you cross the ER229. Drawing ever closer to Cabo Girão, enjoy the splendid views of the coast above **Caldeira**. Some sheer drops are encountered just before you curl right through the Cabo Girão tunnel at **Cruz da Caldeira** (**③**; **1h55min**), but they are protected by railings. (You may wish to take a detour here to Cabo Girão; see notes for Short walk 1 on page 54.) It only takes three minutes to walk through this tunnel and it *can* be managed without a

The splendid vineyards below the church at Garachico

torch, since the path is wide and the roof is high. Now Cabo Girão has disappeared, and you're in the **Ribeira da Quinta Grande**. At **2h10min** the levada skirts the river bridge below the ER229. *Before you reach the parapet*, climb steps up right to the main road (**4**). (*Short walk 2 begins here on the west side of the road*, where the signposted levada is covered with concrete for a short distance; deduct 2h10min from times below.)

At **2h25min** count the second church — at **Quinta Grande** — as you continue along another high and narrow stretch, parallel with the ER229. Soon come to a spot that's exceptionally lovely in the autumn: stately pillars of pine and sweet chestnut stand proud in iron-rich soil, and the forest is alive with pink belladonna lilies. Further on, the houses are festooned with dahlias and the aroma of wood fires is in the air. On roof-tops, marrows and beans almost strangle the charming chimneys.

Count the church of Campanário off to the west and start heading up the valley of the **Ribeira do Campanário**, golden with gorse and broom in spring. Some very severe drops to the left are secured by iron railings (**3h10min**). Soon you see the ER229 above Campanário — the square-shaped U-turn is very easily recognised. Cross the Ribeira do Campanário by a tank and tiered sluice at the Covão levada tunnel, which draws water from tributaries of the Soccoridos (**3h35min**).

Continue through the wooded heights above **Campanário** and in 10 minutes (**5**; **3h45min**) you'll cross a dirt track. (*If you are doing Short walk 2, leave here: descend the track — which quickly becomes a road — to the ER229, where you'll find a bus stop and a bar/shop.*)

Those continuing on the levada will cross a concrete lane and then, beyond a large circular tank, the asphalt road to Lugar da Serra at **4h10min**. A FOOTBALL PITCH (**6**) is just below the levada, on the east side of the road. Eight minutes later pass a lovely little ruin on the right, with a grassy *poio* and chestnut trees — a delightful spot for a break. Soon you enjoy a fine view over the graceful arc of the expressway.

Walk round the fence of a large waterhouse to continue on the levada, then meet the road down to Boa Morte (**7**; **4h35min**; *Short walk 3 comes in here*). Cross the road (the bar/café O Pinheiro is down to the left) and continue past housing and then below a large industrial estate (heavy construction). The levada now runs through a verdant new wood of fast-growing mimosa and eucalyptus, replacing the once-proud pine forest that was destroyed by fires several years ago. Some 12-13 minutes after crossing the Boa Morte road, note a track off left (**8**; **4h48min**). For the moment pass it by; soon, from a CONCRETE PLATFORM (**9**; **5h**), you have magnificent views north and south over the great cleft of the Ribeira Brava, its terraces, poplars, and banana plantations.

This platform makes a lovely picnic spot — or you could carry on for a couple of minutes more, to where you can look across the valley to the Paúl da Serra and up north towards Encumeada (*P6*). This levada flows from far, far north of the viewpoint. (You could easily follow it to Eira do Mourão and the setting shown below or go as far as the first tunnel (1h), but the path will become extremely vertiginous, and there is no protective fencing: a hiker was killed here just before press date. *Experts:* it's 13km/8mi; 4h30min of almost constant 'exposure' — or long tunnels! — from here to the power station at Serra de Água; a torch is essential.)

Return from your viewpoint to the track first passed at 4h48min and descend to **Boa Morte** (**C**; **5h40min**). It's unlikely you'll catch the last bus of the day, so walk down to the ER229 at **Barreiras** (**B**; **6h20min**); the BUS SHELTER is opposite.

Continuing along the levada to Eira do Mourão is highly recommended.

Walk 7: LEVADA DOS TORNOS FROM CURRAL DOS ROMEIROS TO THE SÍTIO DAS QUATRO ESTRADAS

Distance: 27.5km/17mi; 7h30min (but see Short walks below).

Grade, equipment, how to get there and return: see Short walks.

Short walks: This walk breaks conveniently into the four stages described below. We begin at Curral dos Romeiros, to avoid climbing to the levada. If you wish to begin at Monte (🚠) or Babosas (🚠; a small square just east of the Funchal cable car terminus, near the Jardim Botânico cable car terminus; access by *town* 🚌 20, 21, 22 or 🚠), follow the '7' arrows on the map. The path to Curral dos Romeiros leaves Babosas along the walkway to the Jardim Botânico cable car (various signs, including 'Levada dos Tornos'), then descends below the station. *Important:* 350m/yds below Babosas, **there is a critical choice of paths (❶)**. *If you have a head for heights, keep ahead (left) on the earthen path for 'Levada dos Tornos'. If not, curl sharp right downhill on the main trail with street lights;* it will take you to Romeiros (❷), where you can pick up Short walk 1 (page 60). The path ahead/left rises gently for just over 15 minutes to join the levada at the point where it emerges from a long tunnel and rounds the upper João Gomes Valley — a truly primeval setting. While there are some protective railings, those prone to vertigo may find the going very tough!

1 Curral dos Romeiros — Palheiro Ferreiro. 6km/3.7mi; 1h30min.
● Easy, *but see notes page 60.* Stout shoes, sunhat, picnic, water. *Town* 🚌 29 to Curral dos Romeiros (❷). To return: 1) end at the Hortensia tea house and return on *town* 🚌 47; 2) follow the ER205 200m down to the right for 🚌 129/77/*town* 🚌 37; 3) *cross* the ER205 (❹) and follow Short walk 2 to the next road: the terminus for *town* 🚌 36/36A and a bar are 60m downhill, opposite an entrance to the Palheiro Gardens (open 09.30-16.30 Mon-Fri, except holidays; bar/restaurant). Notes page 60.

2 Palheiro Ferreiro — Camacha. 5.7km/3.5mi; 1h40min. ● Easy, but there is a very awkward tunnel (❺; 10 minutes) and a stiffish climb of 100m/330ft from Ribeirinha up to Camacha. Stout shoes (boots preferable), sunhat, picnic, water and a *good torch* for each member of the party. *Town* 🚌 37 or 🚌 129 or 77 to the ER205 (❹) at Palheiro Ferreiro; ask for 'Levada dos Tornos'. Return from Camacha (❻) on 🚌 129 or 77 (or from Nogueira on 🚌 110 or 114). Notes begin on page 61.

3 Camacha — Lombo Grande. 7km/4.3mi; 1h40min. ● :: Expert; *you must be sure-footed; danger of vertigo:* the path is very narrow in places and dangerous if storm-damaged; you may have to walk *through* waterfalls. Equipment as for Short walk 2 above, plus extra fleece, long trousers, windproof in cool weather, whistle. *Don't forget the torches!* 🚌 129 or 77 to Camacha (❻); return on 🚌 60 (the stop is on the ER206, just below Lombo Grande; ❼) or walk 1km uphill to Boqueirão (🚌 85, 110) or 1.6km uphill to Águas Mansas (🚌 77). Notes begin on page 64.

4 Lombo Grande — Sítio das Quatro Estradas. ● :: 11.5km/7.1mi; 3h. Grade and equipment as Short walk 3, *but this stretch of levada is even more vertiginous* and there is a tiring climb of 150m/500ft to the Sítio das Quatro Estradas (❾). Access: 🚌 60 (ask for 'Levada dos Tornos, Lombo Grande'; ❼). From the bus stop, walk north up the ER206 for one minute to the levada. Or take 🚌 77 to Águas Mansas or 🚌 85 or 110 to Boqueirão, then walk down to the levada (1.6km below Águas Mansas, 1km below Boqueirão). Notes begin on page 64.

Alternative walks: By referring to the maps on pages 60-63, you can put together some interesting combinations with Walk 8, 9 or 10. You shouldn't have any difficulty, either, reversing Short walks 1, 2 or 3 (the descent to the levada on Short walk 4 is very steep in reverse.

The touring map gives you a good overview of the **Levada dos Tornos**. Inaugurated in 1966, it is Madeira's most important levada, with 106km (66mi) of main channels. Water collected from three chief sources in the north flows to the power station at Fajã da Nogueira. (You can explore the northern reaches of the Tornos on Walks 23 and 24.)

From the power station at Fajã da Nogueira (Walk 24) the levada flows through a very long tunnel (there are 16km/10mi of tunnels on the Tornos!) to the south of the island. It emerges into the open in the upper reaches of the João Gomes Valley, north of Curral dos Romeiros, and then meanders on to irrigate more than 100,000 outlets between Funchal and Santa Cruz. And it is this southern run of the Tornos that we describe in the walk. From a height of 600m (almost 2000ft), the hustle and bustle of life at sea level seems very far away — it's like overflying the south coast in a balloon.

Before starting note that Short walk 1 was devastated in the August 2016 fires and still utterly grim at press date, the worst stretch being around Choupana. We include it as access to Walk 8 and because the tea houses are so popular!

Start Short walk 1 at **Curral dos Romeiros**:* ask the bus driver for 'Levada', and you will be dropped off by steps leading up to it (❷; officially, it's stop S3A). At the top of the steps turn right on the covered levada; you'll soon see it in

*If you come from Monte or Babosas by the trail with street lights, take the middle road as you come into the village: walk past a building with a flagpole *and* the steps just past it. Climb the *next* set of steps up left to the levada (covered by concrete). If you come on the higher levada path you will cross a road. Descend steps on the far side, turn left at the bottom, walk past a building with a flagpole and proceed as three lines above.

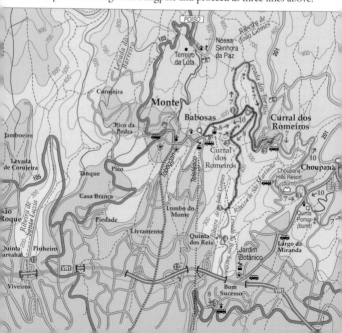

full flow. If you must detour round the burnt-out CHOUPANA HILLS RESORT (**20min**), it will be signed. Otherwise, if you can stay on the levada, you will cross a road (**❸**; **35min**); it leads south to the JARDIM BOTÂNICO). A CHAPEL survives on your right; it belonged to the burnt-out QUINTA DO POMAR. (The island's 'national' football stadium, just above, miraculously survived.) Then you cross another road. In about **1h** you cross a road by a STOP FOR TOWN BUS 47 (**ⓑ**); 200m/yds further on, steps lead up left to the HORTENSIA tea house. Cross the ER201 (**ⓒ**; **1h10min**) and three minutes later pass above the JASMIN tea house. In **1h30min** you reach the ER205 (**❹**). Approach *carefully* — traffic roars round the blind bend to the left. End the walk here (there is a BUS STOP 200m/yds downhill to the right) or cross the road and follow Short walk 2 below for five minutes — to the next, quieter road, then walk 60m/yds downhill to the TERMINUS FOR BUSES 36 AND 36A, in front of a BAR and opposite an entrance to the PALHEIRO GARDENS.

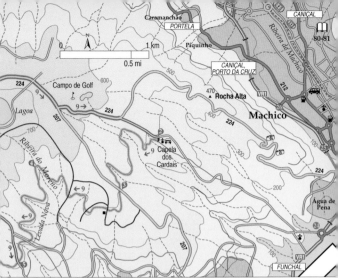

Short walk 2 begins at the **Levada dos Tornos** BUS STOP on the ER205 (④). The levada is 100m/yds downhill from the 'official' stop; it runs just at the left of a small road called RAMPA DO PALHEIRO FERREIRO. Heading east, you look over the golf course and reservoirs at **Palheiro Ferreiro** to the Desertas Islands. In three minutes you pass a school and builders' merchants on the right; a fenced stadium is above you, on the left. Cross a road and rejoin the levada by turning *sharp* left. Fragrant mimosa and eucalyptus grace the next stretch.

In **20min** you come to a TUNNEL (⑤;10min to pass). *Watch your head: the roof is low and jagged.* (Earthen steps at the right of the tunnel lead up to a road at **Pinheirinho**, with bar/shop and TERMINUS FOR BUS 37 (④), but the descent back to the levada can be very slippery. This route is highlighted in violet on the map, if you don't fancy the tunnel.)

After crossing a road, you enter the valley of the **Ribeira do Caniço**, sprinkled with apple blossom in spring. On the far side of the valley *leave* the levada before it goes through the next tunnel: 150m/yds before a small white waterhouse on the left, take steps up left (signed to 'Camacha'). Join a road and follow it to the right uphill through **Nogueira**. In the large housing estate, ignore all crossroads and keep ahead uphill. Pass a stop sign and walk ahead past the TERMINUS FOR BUS 114 (ⓒ; where you could end the walk), to a T-junction with the ER205 (Caniço road; **1h05min**).

Turn left but, a minute uphill, at the Laboratório Agricola, turn right on TRAVESSA JOÃO CLAUDIO NOBREGA. Cross a road, then go under the main CAMACHA VE5 ROAD BRIDGE and down into **Ribeirinha** (where there is a stop for bus 111). Unless you want to stay on the levada, follow the road across a BRIDGE (ⓣ) and up out of Ribeirinha, to a T-junction. Go left uphill here* (CAMINHO FONTE CONCELOS). Ignore a road off right; keep left on Caminho Fonte Concelos and rise steeply, to cross the Camacha bypass. Passing a modern church on your right, you come into **Camacha** by the village square (**6**; Achada da Camacha; **1h40min**). The BUS STOP is straight ahead; the ESTALAGEM DO RELÓGIO is to your right.

Start Short walk 3 facing the CAFÉ/ESTALAGEM DO RELÓGIO in **Camacha**'s square (**6**; Achada da Camacha). Descend the road at the right of the café (signposted to Funchal; a modern church is to your left). Ignore a small road off right, cross the bypass road and continue down the road almost directly opposite (CAMINHO FONTE CONCELOS). In **7min** fork right and then look left for a fine view over the Porto Novo. A few minutes later, turn left at a T-junction. Watch for where the road crosses the **Levada dos Tornos** (**6**; by a small parking bay; **14min**) and turn left on the levada.

Having passed a house with a pretty palm tree and a road on the right (**23min**), you come to a tunnel under the Salgados road a minute later. You'll need your torch, although it takes only three minutes to get through. Another tunnel is met in **40min** (two minutes; again you'll need your torch). Beyond this tunnel there is a possibility of vertigo for, although the levada path is very adequate, there is no protective fencing, and the drops are severe — perhaps 50m/150ft. Often waterfalls cascade onto the path as well, and you may get soaked. Watch out, too, for the concrete blocks in the path, supporting the pipe carrying some of the water. Still, we hope you will manage this part of the walk in the lower part of the **Ribeira do Porto Novo** because it is one of the most beautiful parts of the Tornos. Suddenly birds and cascades are singing everywhere. In **50min** the levada makes a U-turn high in the valley, below some POOLS (**6**). The waterfall shown opposite crashes into the river; all else is stillness. This is an idyllic picnic spot.

Eight minutes from the pools you pass a dyke on the right and a *palheiro*. Pass through the third and shortest tunnel (**1h**), before skirting round a tunnel with 'windows' at about **1h10min** (be sure to climb up steps beyond this tunnel to rejoin the Tornos; the levada continuing straight ahead runs down to Gaula). This is another lovely picnic spot (**P**7a). Across the valley you can see the village of Salgados, dribbling down the ridge. All too soon, you reach a RESERVOIR at

---

*To continue on the levada, take the path by a signpost 'Levada dos Tornos' (it *may* be hidden in greenery) on your right, some 200m/yds past the bridge. The path passes to the left of the (ruined) beautiful rose-painted house with a timbered balcony shown on page 65. Five minutes off the road, you reach the levada in a minute: turn left. Pick up the notes for Short walk 3 at the 14min-point (where the walk joins the levada just above a small parking bay).

Along the Tornos (clockwise): old house at Nogueira, waterfall at the head of the Porto Novo Valley, flower-filled channel near Curral dos Romeiros and rose-painted house at Ribeirinha (see footnote opposite).

Lombo Grande. Beyond it is the ER206 (**7**; just over **1h30min**). Turn right and descend for under a minute to the BUS STOP.

Short walk 4 begins where the ER206 crosses the levada at **Lombo Grande** (**7**). Head east; in under **10min** you have good views over the airport and São Lourenço Point. After **20min** you pass through a very short tunnel (no torch is needed, but it is very low: watch your head!) and come out in the **Ribeira da Boaventura** (**P7**b). While the Porto Novo is our favourite part of the Tornos in spring, in summer the Boaventura Valley (see page 66) takes the prize. The terraces are golden with wheat, and the levada paths are aglow with blue and white agapanthus — so tall and thick that they are almost like hedgerows. Most walkers will have no difficulty following the levada for a good 20 minutes past the tunnel, but then the way becomes vertiginous, as it delves into a very deep tributary, the **Ribeira dos Vinháticos**. By **50min** you reach the head of this stream (**i**). The next, smaller tributary, is a basin full of willow. In just over **1h35min** you pass a waterhouse on the left; beyond it is an asphalt road. Two minutes later a second asphalt road is crossed (**i**; **1h40min**). Both lead up to the ER110 at João Frino, if you're short of time and trying to catch bus 77. Beyond the second road you delve into the upper reaches of a new valley — the **Ribeira de Santa Cruz**. Ignore all the cobbled trails and paths crossing the levada during the next 45 minutes or so; civilisation seems very far away, as you enter an emerald wilderness.

Then suddenly, at **2h25min**, the LEVADA ENDS (**8**). Unbelievable! How can this magnificent watercourse, which has carried you through the most beautiful valleys in the southeast, have abandoned you without warning? Its waters shoot out into a tank some 200m/650ft below, to feed the Levada Nova (see Walk 9). A pipe coming in from the Levada da

Serra (Walk 10) runs down and over to the *lagoa* (reservoir) above Santo da Serra.

Walk back along the levada. In two minutes you pass a narrow signposted path on the left (**k**; it leads to Walk 9, but we do not recommend this steep and slippery *descent*). There is also a sign pointing right to Santo da Serra but, again, it's not the route we recommend — although it emerges near our route. Four minutes later (450m/yds from the tank), turn right up cobbled steps (**l**). When you rise up to fields, walk towards the electricity wires ahead, keeping to the left of the plots. Follow the path to a cobbled track below the wires: this is the gorgeous hamlet of **Serra das Ameixieiras**. Go left uphill (past the gated entrance to a *quinta*), to an asphalted crossroads(**m**). Here go straight ahead.* When two tarred roads join from the left, keep straight on (right), rising to the ER110 at the **Sítio das Quatro Estradas** (**o; 3h**). Your BUS SHELTER is diagonally right across the road.

*If you turn right here, you can follow the tarred Caminho da Pereira 30 minutes to Santo da Serra (see violet route on the map). You first skirt the grounds of the mysterious *quinta*, overgrown with luxuriant vegetation. For a short time in the 1800s it was home to a young Scottish doctor, Robert Reid Kalley, esteemed by the islanders for his near-miraculous cures. But he was also a Protestant, and when the authorities could no longer tolerate his incessant proselytising, he had to flee the island dressed as a woman.) At any forks, be sure to keep to the same signposted road. You cross the Ribeira Serra de Água, pass a few isolated *quintas*, then rise through housing to Santo da Serra (**o**).

Map pages 60-61; photo page 39 (right)

Distance: 4.4km/2.7mi; 1h45min

Grade: ● ❚❚ Expert; *you must be sure-footed*; ***danger of vertigo***: a very steep descent of 400m/1300ft (mostly on steps), on a partly eroded, often unprotected path. *Not suitable after rain*, when it is *very* slippery.

Equipment: walking boots, long trousers, water; extra fleece and windproof in cool weather, walking stick(s)

How to get there: 🚡 or town 🚌 22 to Babosas
To return: town 🚌 7, 29, 30, 33, 34A, 36 or 47 from Bom Sucesso

One of the things that has always amazed us about Madeira is how close you can be to dense housing yet come upon a primeval landscape just around a fold in the hillside. This walk is a perfect example; it explores the 'Green Corridor' created by the awesome João Gomes Valley.

Start out at **Babosas** (○): go down the walkway past the Jardim Botânico cable car (various signs, including 'BOM SUCESSO'). At an important fork after 350m/yds (❶; **7min**), curl sharp right downhill*, keeping to the main trail with street lights ('Levada do Bom Sucesso'). Follow this across a BRIDGE over the **João Gomes River**, rise up the far side and then fork right (❸; sign: 'LEVADA DO BOM SUCESSO'; **13min**).

A log-stepped path now takes you *very* steeply down the east side of the Ribeira de João Gomes, along the 'Green Corridor'. The dark forest of pine and eucalyptus is brightened by a myriad of mimosas and wild flowers in spring. Ten-15 minutes down, a CLEARING makes a pleasant place to pause. Two minutes past the clearing, at a T-junction, the main path goes left (❷). But first go *right,* following red paint lettering on a rock: 'waterfall 200 m'. It's not difficult to scramble down to the pools below the WATERFALL and enjoy a paddle.

Back at the T-junction, go straight ahead, contouring for a while. Then the stepped path drops very steeply again. Ten minutes down from the junction a RED ARROW points right to a non-existent path: it's there to alert you to a fork a bit further on, where the main path drops steeply to the right and you ignore a level path straight ahead. Crossing a high, narrow BRIDGE (❸; **1h05min**), you are finally following the elusive **Levada do Bom Sucesso**, with fantastic views to the expressway, the cable cars and the Bay of Funchal. Ten minutes later another BRIDGE (❹) is crossed; just before it, another redpainted rock alerts you to a WATERFALL 300 m to the right.

Then you pass below the EXPRESSWAY (**1h20min**), where the path is very wet and slippery, even in summer. Meeting a T-junction, walk straight ahead on Rua Dr Antonio Costa, past a side-entrance to the ORCHID GARDEN on the left. The road curls right, down to the main road at **Bom Sucesso**. A BUS SHELTER is to your left (❺; **1h45min**), a BAR to the right.

*Or first go left: see the 'Short walk' notes at the top of page 59.

Walk 9: SANTO DA SERRA • LEVADA NOVA • SÍTIO DAS QUATRO ESTRADAS

Map pages 62-63   **Distance:** 14km/8.7mi; 4h

Grade: ● ‡‡ easy-moderate, with a steep climb of 250m/820ft at the end of the walk. You must be sure-footed and have a head for heights (*danger of vertigo*). *Note:* This walk is best done between early May and October and in the direction described (see caption opposite).

Equipment: stout shoes (walking boots preferable), long trousers, sunhat, picnic, water; extra fleece and windproof in cool weather

How to get there: 🚌 20, 77 or 78 to Santo da Serra (or 🚗: 32° 43.462'N, 16° 49.177'W). To avoid a long walk on tarmac, take a 🚕 *taxi* from there to the Capela dos Cardais, where the levada walk starts (deduct 40min). *To return:* 🚌 77 from the Sítio das Quatro Estradas (or same bus or 🚗 from Santo da Serra; add 15min)

Short walk: Santo da Serra — Levada Nova — Sítio das Quatro Estradas (or Santo da Serra). ● ‡‡ 7km/4.3mi; 2h25min. Grade, equipment, access/return as main walk. Follow the main walk for 6min, but at the Quinta da Paz (❶) fork *right*. Descend this lane (tar, then concrete) 3km to the levada (keeping right at a fork 2.5km downhill), then pick up the main walk at ❺ (the 2h20min-point. Includes the loveliest part of the walk.

Alternative end to main or short walk: ● ‡‡ From the water tank (❻) go back a short way *past* the steps on the right down to the bridge/ford (❼), then climb concrete steps on the *left* (sign: 'Santa da Serra'). At the top take the ongoing track up to a tarred lane (❾) and turn left. Now it's 1km to Santo da Serra via the Quinta da Paz (saving about 80m of ascent).

If you've walked the Levada dos Tornos from start to finish, wouldn't you think that you'd seen the best of the Santa Cruz Valley? After all, the Tornos is 100m/330ft higher than the Levada Nova. Wouldn't you expect it to be greener, more vertiginous, more beautiful and more exciting than this lower levada? You are in for a surprise!

Start out at the CHURCH in **Santo da Serra** (○). Follow the ER224 southeast, past the park and a hotel on your left. Ignore a bypass road coming in from the right at the roundabout but, a few paces further on, at the Y-fork in front of the QUINTA DA PAZ (❶; **6min**) bear left. *(But go right for the Short walk).* You pass the GOLF COURSE on your left and the *lagoa* (reservoir) on the conical hill above right. Some 400m past the golfers' clubhouse, at another fork, go left ('MACHICO'). After 750m, at another fork, go right towards 'ÁGUA DE PENA'. Ten minutes' descent brings you the CAPELA DOS CARDAIS, on your right (❷; **40min**). Climb the steps between the chapel and a large water tank to join the **Levada Nova**.

As you head west, the way is graced by *Senecio,* passion flowers … and blackberry thorns. You cross the ER207 running south to the airport at **1h18min**. Three minutes later, beyond a track, you come to a sizeable (but apparently defunct) PIGGERY. A couple of stone-laid trails cross your way not far beyond here. Having rounded the **Ribeira do Moreno** (❹) and crossed a concrete road, in **2h20min** you meet

Hidden in a glen of fuchsias are some pretty rock pools in the upper reaches of the Ribeira de Santa Cruz — a delightful spot to take a break, before heading back to Santo da Serra's highlands. The bridge is often washed away in storms and replaced by a ford, which may be impassable after heavy rains. Since the levada itself is also often blocked by fallen trees after high winds — and indeed may be signposted as officially closed for that reason —, this walk is best saved for the summer months!

another concrete road *(the Short walk rejoins here)*. Cross the road; the levada is appreciably wider now, as you head up into the **Ribeira de Santa Cruz**.

This stretch is guaranteed to delight even the most jaded levada-walker. Masses upon masses of blue and white agapanthus dance along the curves of the channel, a waterfall bursts upon the scene and then, in **2h55min**, you come to an emerald-green fern-covered grotto. But there is more to come: river pools shimmer down to the left, and soon you're in a glen of wild fuchsias. It's all too wonderful to last, and it doesn't. Almost at once the source of the levada is met at a tank, where overspill water pours in from the Levada dos Tornos above. A pipe (some of it underground) carries water here from the Levada da Serra (Walk 10) as well. Another pipe, this one visible, runs up to the *lagoa* above Santo da Serra.

From the water catchment, retrace your steps for just over a minute, then descend steps to a BRIDGE/FORD (**7**) over the river. Climb the path on the far side *(turning sharp left some 3m/yds uphill)*. You struggle up to the **Levada dos Tornos** in 15 minutes. Turn right and follow it for two minutes, to where it ends and spills over into the water tank you've just left (**8**; **3h25min**). Turn back here and use the notes in the last paragraph on page 66, to climb to the **Sítio das Quatro Estradas** (**O**; **4h**), or see the footnote on the same page to go direct to Santo da Serra, if you've left your car there.

Walk 10: LEVADA DA SERRA: FROM CHOUPANA TO PORTELA

Map begins on pages 60-61, continues on pages 62-63, and ends on pages 80-81; photographs pages 21, 82-83

Distance: See introduction and 'The entire length' below.

Grade: ● easy throughout *if done in stages*, but there may be an initial climb to the levada (some buses now cross it, or friends may play taxi for you; see map and notes). *Note that mountain bikers are now using this route.*

Equipment: stout shoes, sunhat, picnic, water; extra fleece and windproof in cool weather (especially for the stretch north of Camacha)

How to get there and return: See Short walks 1-5 below.

Short walks: See 1-5 below (all except 'The entire length' are easy).

The Levada da Serra is one of the easiest and most popular walking routes on Madeira. Since the trail is well signposted, and there is little chance of getting lost, we don't describe the walk in detail. Instead, we tell you how to join the walk at convenient points and do the suggested segments in both directions. *Don't* expect to see water in this levada — it has either been diverted to the Tornos (Walk 7) or piped (in which case the channel itself may be filled in). Nor are there many far-reaching views; trees line much of the route. Enjoy instead the flora (hydrangeas, gorse, lilies, rhododendrons) and the pleasant shade of eucalyptus, oaks and laurels.

The **Levada da Serra** is some 27km/17mi long, from the **Lamaceiros** waterhouse above Portela to its end at **Choupana** (fire-ravaged in August 2016). It can be done in one fell swoop, but it breaks conveniently into five short walks.

The entire length: Choupana — Lamaceiros — Portela. 30km/ 18.6mi; 8h. Grade: ● moderate (on account of the length). Take *town* 🚌 47 to the Centro Hípico (just west of ❸). Continue north along the ER201 for 1.3km, then climb a steep cobbled trail on the right (❍; Caminho do Pico do Infante, opposite the Caminho do Meio). In under eight minutes, a short cobbled path on the right leads to the (dry) levada, which may be hidden by tall grass. Follow the levada to the Lamaceiros waterhouse, then pick up Walk 25 to descend to Portela (🚌 53 or 78). Alternatively, leave at the Santo da Serra waterhouse: descend the track on the south side of this waterhouse to the ER110 and turn right, then left into Santo da Serra for 🚌 20, 77 or 78 (27km/16.7mi; under 8h). If you do this long walk from Portela (see Short walk 5 below), see notes for Short walk 1 to descend from Choupana. *Note: The levada is covered by a road in the Porto Novo Valley; the short walks omit this stretch.*

Short walks

1 Choupana — Achadinha. ● 7.6km/4.7mi; 2h10min. Access as 'The entire length'. After crossing the ER203 to Poiso (❶), continue for another 3.5km to Achadinha (❷), where 🚌 111 stops beside the levada. *To walk this leg in reverse,* take 🚌 111 to the 'Levada da Serra' bus stop at Achadinha (❷). Follow the levada west, crossing the ER203 to Poiso (❶). When the levada ends at a T-junction with a steep cobbled trail (at Choupana), turn left down to the ER201 (❍; 6min). To catch *town* 🚌 47, turn left: in under 15 minutes you'll come to the 'Centro Hípico' bus stop. Or carry on to the Jardim Botânico (35min), the cable car at Babosas, or Monte (2h): go straight over the ER201. Descend the steep Caminho do Meio ahead 2km to the Jardim Botânico or descend only 500m/yds and then turn right on the Levada dos Tornos (❸). Beyond the burnt-out Choupana Hills Resort, at Curral dos Romeiros (❷; 45min), steps take you down left off the levada, to avoid a building with a flagpole. Turn right on the road, walking *below* the building with a flagpole. When the road reverts to path, follow street lights all the way to Babosas (❍; viewpoint, cable cars to the Jardim Botânico or Funchal) or Monte (❶).

2   Paradise Valley — Camacha. ● 6km/3.7mi; 1h40min. Take 🚌 129 or 77 to junction of the ER205 and ER203 at Vale Paraíso (❍; the 'Estrada para Carreiras' bus stop). Climb the ER203 towards Poiso to the levada (❶; 10min) and turn right. Ignore any forks down right. Go straight over a crossroads signposted 'Levada da Serra' at Achadinha (❷). At the next crossroads (❸; Caminho Municipal da Portela; 1h20min), turn right downhill to Camacha (❻; 🚌 129, 77). *To reverse the walk,* take 🚌 129 to Camacha (❻) and walk north up the ER110 from Camacha's square, then climb a road on the left, just past the old church (Caminho Municipal da Portela; walkers' signposts on the left). At the levada crossing (❸; under 15min), go left. When you come to the crossing Poiso road (❶; ER203) turn down left to the ER205 (❍; 🚌 129, 77). Or carry on to Choupana (❍); for transport from there, see Short walk 1.

3   Águas Mansas — Sítio das Quatro Estradas. ● 6km/3.7mi; 1h40min. Take 🚌 77 to Águas Mansas, or 🚌 110 to Boqueirão (from where you must walk 0.6km uphill to the ER110; add 10min). From the joining of the ER206 and the ER110 (❹), walk 100m north towards Santo da Serra, then turn left up a road. Just before a forestry house (where the road reverts to track), go left on a path at the left of the rushing Levada do Pico. Cross a track and continue up to the dry Levada da Serra (❺; 10min). Turn right and follow it as far as the ER202 to Poiso (❼); there turn down right to the ER110 to catch 🚌 77 at the Sítio das Quatro Estradas (❍; 'the four roads'). *To do this stretch in reverse,* join the levada as in Short walk 4 and turn left. When you reach the noisy Levada do Pico (❺), follow it to the left downhill, to a track. Turn left, then turn right down another track, to the ER110 at Águas Mansas (❹; 🚌 77).

4   Sítio das Quatro Estradas — Santo da Serra. ● 8km/5mi; 2h 20min. Take 🚌 77 to the Sítio das Quatro Estradas (❍; 'See-tee-oh dahs Kwa-troh Esh-trah-dahsh'). Climb the ER202 towards Poiso. Just beyond a huge piggery (15min), turn right on the levada (❼; *P*10). About 1h15min later, you cross a track and come to the Santo da Serra water-house (❽). Enjoy its charming gardens, then return to the track and descend past a café/trout fishing to the ER110 (❾; 25min). Turn right downhill, then left into Santo da Serra (❍; 20min; 🚌 20, 77, 78). *To do this stretch in reverse,* join the levada as in Short walk 5 and turn left. Reaching the crossing ER202 to Poiso (❼), turn down left to the ER110 (❍; 🚌 77).

5   Santo da Serra — Portela. ● 7.6km/4.7mi; 2h35min. Take 🚌 20, 77 or 78 to Santo da Serra church (❍). Walk 500m west to the ER110 and turn right uphill for 300m/yds. Then turn left on a road/track (❍) past a café/trout fishing, rising 100m/330ft to the Santo da Serra water-house (❽). Turn right, walk to the Lamaceiros waterhouse (❸), then follow Walk 25 (page 105) to Portela (❍). *To begin at Portela,* take 🚌 53 or 78 to Portela (❍). Cross the road and climb steps up to a viewpoint on the ER110. Then walk 100m south up that road and climb steps on the right (at a PR10 sign). Follow the Levada da Portela 200m/650ft uphill to Lamaceiros (❸). Walk south on the Levada da Serra to the Santo da Serra waterhouse (❽), then descend as in Short walk 4 above.

Walk 11: LEVADA DO CANIÇAL FROM MAROÇOS TO THE CANIÇAL TUNNEL

Map pages 80-81

Distance: 12km/7.4mi; 2h40min   **Grade:** ● easy, but a bit long

Equipment: stout shoes, sunhat, long-sleeved shirt, picnic, water; extra fleece and windproof in cool weather

How to get there: 🚌 208 (or 156; see timetable page 141) to the bar 'A Calçadinha' at the start of the levada above Maroços

To return: 🚌 113 from the Pico do Facho bus stop

Short walk: Caniçal tunnel — Boca do Risco — Ribeira Seca. ● 6.5km/ 4mi; 1h45min. Quite easy; ascent of 100m/300ft. 🚌 113 to the Pico do Facho bus stop on the western side of the Caniçal tunnel (**O**). Join the Levada do Caniçal by the waterhouse on the north side of the road and head west. After 35-40min a path crosses the levada (**a**); it rises from a house at the top of the valley (with electricity wires). Follow the path up to the right; it's a 30min climb from here to Boca do Risco (**①**; see pages 79-80; Walk 14). Return the same way and then descend past the house, following the electricity poles down to the road in the valley. Catch 🚌 113RS to Funchal just 50m down the road (**ⓑ**; at 11.00, 13.00 daily, also 14.00, 17.30 Mon-Fri). Or continue to the ER214 (**ⓒ**) for 🚌 113.

Alternative walk: Maroços to Caniçal. ● ⁞⁞ 16km/10mi; 5h05min. Access as above; grade, equipment, return *as Walk 12*. Do the main walk, then continue to Caniçal by following the first half of Walk 12.

The 'mimosa levada' offers an entrancing and easy walk, accessible to most visitors. If you like, you can extend the walk by including a (1h return) detour to Boca do Risco, or you can tack on Walk 12 — going all the way to Caniçal, or just to Pico do Facho and back. In recent years new housing has burgeoned in the lower valleys, but there are still many peaceful pockets of greenery beside the levada.

The walk begins at the BUS STOP opposite the bar **A Calçadinha** at Maroços (**O**). (If approaching by car, see the footnote on page 22.) A walkers' signpost for 'Caniçal' announces the **Levada do Caniçal**, initially covered with concrete. After crossing a steep road in under **10min**, you'll quickly gain the

No habitation disturbs the peace in the upper valleys — as yet!

Terracotta birds keep silent watch over the valley of the Ribeira Grande.

narrow **Ribeira das Cales**, as you walk through the strung-out village of Maroços. Out of this tributary, you pass above a school and then come into the **Ribeira Grande**, crossing the head of the river in **50min** (**❶**). From now on you will encounter fewer dwellings for a time, but the handiwork of the Madeiran farmer is all around. *Palheiros* dot the landscape, mere specks of red and white in the great bowls of greenery. Perhaps you'll meet a youngster bringing home a melon — he puts it into the levada and 'steers' it with a stick … But it is more likely that your only companions will be full-throated frogs singing to their hearts' content.

A short TUNNEL is met at the end of this valley (**1h**; no torch needed) and minutes later a couple of WATERHOUSES perched up beside the levada. Then the walk turns into the heavily populated valley of the Ribeira Seca. Take heart! Before pressing on to civilisation we delve into the remote tributary valley shown opposite, the **Ribeira da Noia**. Utterly peaceful, it is still the most beautiful of them all. By now it has become obvious why we call this the 'mimosa levada'! All year round these golden trees will frame your photographs.

After crossing a stream at the head of the Noia Valley and passing a BAR (**❷**) on the left, all too soon you regain the great cornucopia of the **Ribeira Seca**. Linger a while beneath some trees; there's a feast for the eyes all around you. From here you can see Machico and the Desertas Islands glimmering in the sun. You cross the main river at a narrow U-turn; about eight minutes later, notice a wide path crossing the levada (**❸**; **2h**). It comes up from a house and electricity wires. This path leads north to Boca do Risco (1h return; notes pages 79-80; Short walk and Walk 14).

Soon you come upon some gorgeous grassy terraces (**P**11), before the way heads back into shade. You cross a road rising to more cultivated terraces over 100m/350ft higher up and then, just past a handful of houses, a WATERHOUSE with brick trellises beside the ER214 marks the end of the walk (**❹**; **2h40min**). The Caniçal road tunnel is to the left. Catch a bus 30m/yds downhill to the right (the Pico do Facho BUS STOP) or at a pleasant watering hole a further 150m downhill — the Bar Levada Nova (with BUS STOP). Better still, if you're properly shod and have a head for heights, climb the Pico do Facho road opposite, to tackle Walk 12!

Walk 12: PICO DO FACHO — CANIÇAL CIRCUIT

Map pages 76-77   **Distance:** 9.8km/6mi; 3h40min

Grade: ● ‡‡ moderate; overall ascents/descents of about 300m/1000ft; you must be sure-footed and have a head for heights (*danger of vertigo*).

Equipment: walking boots, sunhat, long-sleeved shirt, long trousers, picnic, water

How to get there and return: 🚌 113 to/from the Caniçal tunnel: alight at the western end and return from the eastern end. 🚗 By car, park at the side of the road to Pico do Facho (32° 43.970'N, 16° 45.855'W).

Short walks: ● ‡‡ Do either half of the main walk, ending at or starting from the church in Caniçal (32° 44.262'N, 16° 44.280'W). Grade/equipment as above. About 1h30min.

This invigorating hike first takes you high above the sea, with fine views to São Lourenço. You cross grassy terraces veined with old stone walls and then follow an narrow, often precipitous path — once it was a wide mule trail serving the now mostly abandoned terraces. The second half of the walk follows a narrow levada through mimosas and along sunny slopes, before making a dramatic descent to the ER214.

Start out at the **Pico do Facho** BUS STOP on the west side of the CANIÇAL TUNNEL (**○**). Climb the road towards the peak. Electricity pylons will guide you from here to Caniçal: *take note of them!* The FIRST PYLON (**❶**) comes up just before the peak (**20min**): leave the road here and walk left on a track (just opposite a narrow trail rising up from Machico). At a Y-fork, bear left; the right-hand track runs to a ramshackle shed. Your left fork immediately becomes a path which passes well above the SECOND PYLON and takes you straight to the THIRD PYLON (**40min**). Here, on a ridge between the **Ilhéu** and **Pejal** streams, you enjoy first views of Caniçal.

Now the path unexpectedly turns *inland*. Go left up bedrock and after 20 paces fork right. Ten minutes later (**52min**) the FOURTH PYLON is about 150m/yds ahead of you. *Watch out here* (**❷**). Do *not* follow the path towards this pylon, even if you see an arrow pointing left. The path you want (not easily seen at first) turns off right and runs about 20m/60ft *below* the pylon, rounding it on the sea side, zigzagging and dropping considerably (*follow the red paint dots and take the upper path at a small junction*). When you come to the next bedrock area at a precipice (**1h**), *the path bends sharply to the left.* You overlook Caniçal here. Ten minutes from this precipice, you pass to the left of the FIFTH PYLON (**1h15min**), from where the end of the walk is in view. Looking inland, you spot a beautiful old humpback footbridge over the **Natal** stream below. The path takes you down to it — a scramble involving all fours. Once over the BRIDGE (**❸**; **1h25min**), take the tarmac road down to the seafront. On the far side of the BAR and toilets, follow the seafront promenade left, past the WHALING MUSEUM (**❹**) at **Caniçal**.

74

Turn up the third street on the left, rising to the OLD CHURCH (**1h40min**; bus stop). Head east from the church on the main street, then take the second left turn; Caniçal's large, newer church (with a clock) is ahead on the right. Cross straight over the main road to Baía da Abra; a café will be on your left (**⑤**; **2h**). Climb the road opposite, after 600m passing a WATER DEPOSIT on the right. The asphalt ends at a white-walled CEMETERY on the left. Walk past it on the unsurfaced road; you'll soon see the levada running in the gutter at the left and can walk beside it.

After another 700m/yds, the narrow **Levada do Caniçal** curves left (**⑥**), away from the dirt road (which continues straight on) and enters a wood full of mimosas. Soon you pass a narrower levada rushing down to the left (**2h30min**). Beyond a crossing track, a grassy verge affords a splendid view back down over Caniçal and to an idyllic pink farmhouse surrounded by its beautifully planted plots, the whole framed by a wreath of yellow mimosas. You're heading into a deep tributary of the **Ribeira do Serrado**. A few minutes later you cross the head of this valley on a levada 'BRIDGE' (**⑦**; **2h50min**) with protective railings.

Before long the fine buttress of rock formed by the **Lombo do Vento** and **Pico Judeu** rises on your right. An earthen track joins the levada, and you follow it for a short time, leaving the woods behind for the view shown below. Rejoining the levada, a long sunny stretch takes the ribbon of water through high grasses, with just the odd tree offering welcome shade.

Eventually the watercourse rounds a bend, and now the narrow path runs at the top of a concrete wall high above the ER214 ... and below a quarry (**3h35min**). This is a stunning section of the hike. When you come to a concrete track, descend left to the road, where you can *flag down* a bus (**◉**; **3h40min**). Motorists should turn right and follow the road through the **Caniçal road tunnel** (add 15min; there is a pavement and little traffic these days — or take the bus!).

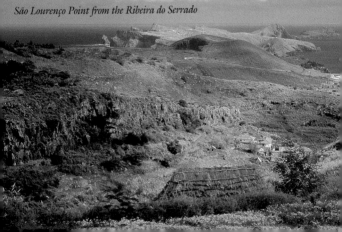

São Lourenço Point from the Ribeira do Serrado

Walk 13: PONTA DE SÃO LOURENÇO

See also photograph page 14   Distance: 8km/5mi; 2h30min

Grade: ● ‡ moderate, with climbs and descents of about 360m/1200ft overall. You must be sure-footed and have a head for heights, despite the well-made paths, boardwalks and steps (which are often covered in pumice and can be slippery). Although all exposed points were protected at time of writing, railings often come down in storms. The hilltop detour at Ponta do Furado is *not suitable when strong winds are blowing*. The walk (PR8) runs through a conservation area laid out by the Department of Forestry and Parks; *keep to the designated paths*.

Equipment: walking boots, long trousers, long-sleeved shirt, sunhat, picnic, water, whistle; fleece and windproof with hood in cool weather, bathing things in summer

How to get there and return: 🚌 to/from Abra Bay, where the ER214 ends (32° 44.584'N, 16° 42.082'W; Car tour 2). Or 🚐 113 to/from Abra Bay (convenient departures; see timetable on page 140 for buses coded 'SL').

Short walk: Abra Bay to the viewpoint over the north coast and return. ● ‡ Easy-moderate, but some people will find the coastal overlook vertiginous, despite the protective railings; 35 minutes return; *especially recommended* as a leg-stretcher on Car tour 2. Stout shoes, sunhat. Access as main walk. Follow the main walk from (**O**) to (**❶**; 20min), then return.

The sun-tanned arm of São Lourenço Point beckons you when you first approach the island by air. Whether you're an experienced walker or just a novice, *do* spend a day out here. Not only are there wonderful flora — including the ice plant *(Mesembryanthemum crystallinum)*, but extraordinary geological formations — basalt intrusions into sandstone, uptilted magma dykes which can be traced across the terrain, metamorphosed sandstone with astonishing textures and colours, and eroded soft rock under basalt tors. You also come

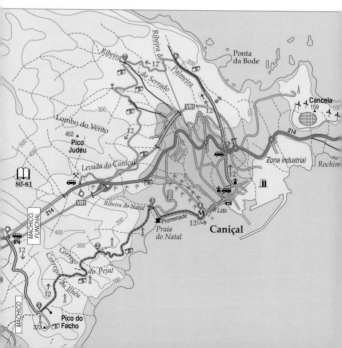

almost face-to-face with the full fury of the Atlantic thrashing against the coast and offshore rocks.

Start the walk where the ER214 ends, at tranquil **Abra Bay** (⚪; **Baía da Abra**; *P*13). You enjoy a fine view of the lighthouse at the end of the point, the eyelet in the lighthouse rock, and the Desertas Islands. Notice the lovely strata opposite you, on the far side of Abra Bay. You can also spot your ongoing route: a trail heading along the arm of the peninsula, on the south side of a hill crowned by the Pedras Brancas trig stone. Follow the sign for the PR8 along the paved path and then a boardwalk. You won't be alone! Go through a gap in an old stone wall (**10min**) and then come upon wonderful views (**15min**; *P*13): to the right is Abra Bay and to the left the north coast headlands as far west as São Jorge. Soon, at a fork, go left on the main trail, ignoring a stepped path down right to the sea and a pebble beach. This main trail brings you to a lip of rock on the north coast in half a minute (❶; **20min**). Here you overlook the magnificent 'sea horse' rocks shown on page 14. The colours are astounding: they seem almost fluorescent, so intense is their purple-red colour as they thrust up from a turquoise-to-indigo sea.

Return to the fork and head left, climbing a stepped and fenced path. *(But for the Short walk, turn right at the fork, back to the car park.)* At a pass (**25min**), be sure to follow the main route sharply left on steps cut into the red tuff — back north to another viewpoint over the north coast 'sea horse' rocks (**30min**) and crossing a saddle where there are more fine views to the left.

Ponta de São Lourenço

Ponta de São Lourenço

Some **40min** into the hike the character of the walk changes completely as you traverse a gentle ridge, and you might like to take a break at a sheltered, grassy spot.

Seven minutes later you come to a stone marker, 'TC/75', at the **Estreito** (Straits; ❷; **47min**), which used to be notoriously difficult to negotiate. From the marker walk 90° left over bedrock, until you overlook the north side of the point. Then follow the sturdy metal fencing, descending in zigzags back to the main path.

From here on the going is really easy and totally exhilarating. Flora are under recovery in this area; *please keep to the paths* defined by the rockery stones. Ahead in the valley is the park rangers' house (Casa do Sardinha). On reaching a fork (❸; **1h**), you can decide whether to make a clockwise or anticlockwise circuit round the house. Whichever route you choose, you will pass two cliff-side VIEWPOINTS looking out to the rest of the peninsula and the Ilhéu do Farol with its lighthouse; these shreds of land are only accessible from the sea. En route you can stop at the little quay (CAIS DO SARDINHA; ❹) for a swim or a picnic. If you like, climb the stepped path to the top of the hill at the **Ponta do Furado** (ⓐ). But despite the fencing, a sign warns that the path is dangerous and the park authorities take no responsibility, so you may prefer to omit this leg of the hike. The 'hill' is only half a hill; beyond the summit there is simply … an abyss.

Everyone takes a picnic break in the shade of palms at the idyllic **Casa do Sardinha** (❺). *Please leave **no** litter in this romantic setting*. The house and quay were built in the early 1900s by a businessman from Funchal called Sardinha.

From here complete the circuit until you rejoin and retrace your outgoing route. You'll be back at the CAR PARK (◯) in about **2h30min**. There is usually a refreshment van here.

78

Walk 14: NORTH COAST PATH: CANIÇAL TUNNEL • BOCA DO RISCO • PORTO DA CRUZ

Distance: 12.5km/7.8mi; 4h

Grade: ● :: moderate ascents of 200m/650ft and descents of 400m/1300ft, but potentially very dangerous: you must be sure-footed and have a head for heights (*danger of vertigo*). *Not suitable* on windy days. The path, 350m/1150ft above the sea, is narrow, often slippery, and *prone to landslides* (usually between Boca do Risco and Espigão Amarelo, below Pico Larano — at times the path is 'officially closed' for just this reason). Organised walking tours use this route regularly, and a frayed cable *usually* protects the worst stretch (but it often comes down in storms). For safety's sake, do the walk with an organised group, or do the Alternative walk.

Equipment: walking boots, sunhat, long trousers, long-sleeved shirt, picnic, water, whistle, fleece, windproof with water

How to get there: 🚌 113 to the Pico do Facho bus stop
To return: 🚌 53 or 78 from Porto da Cruz

Short walk: See Short walk 11 on page 72.

Alternative walk: Larano — Espigão Amarelo — Porto da Cruz. ● :: 7.5km/4.7mi; 2h50min. Moderate, but you must be sure-footed and have a head for heights (*danger of vertigo*). Equipment, return as above. Access: 🚌 53, 78 or 208 (not in the timetables, departs Funchal 10.30 Mo-Fri) to Porto da Cruz, then 🚕 *taxi* to Larano. Or use the map to walk up to Larano — allow about 1h. (🚗: See the map overleaf to drive past Larano — which you may not even notice — and onto a narrow concrete road. Park beside the road just past a goods hoist; 32° 45.692'N, 16° 48.258'W.) Follow the earthen track (❸) running off the concrete road to the coastal path and continue — *provided it is safe* — to Espigão Amarelo, where there is a stone marker (❷; 'JMG'). Or, if there are no landslides, follow it all the way to Boca do Risco (● ::), then join Short walk 11. To return to Porto da Cruz from Larano, pick up the main walk at the 3h20min-point. *See also Alternative walk 15, for a different approach to Larano.*

This is a walk of contrasts. Amble along the Levada do Caniçal, marvelling at the sun-blessed fertility of Madeira's soil. Then climb from the levada to the crest of the coast. Here the wind wakes you to the cruel realities of life

West of Espigão Amarelo your coastal views are framed by pines. Here's where you will see banks of pink belladonna lilies in the autumn.

on the island. The north coast between Boca do Risco and Porto da Cruz is perhaps the quintessence of Madeira — nowhere else on the island can match its rugged, proud beauty in sunlight; few places in the world could match its harsh anger when lashed by storms.

Begin the walk at the PICO DO FACHO BUS STOP on the west side of the CANIÇAL ROAD TUNNEL (○). Cross the road and find the **Levada do Caniçal** (see Walk 11) beside the waterhouse. Follow the levada northwest for about **45min**, until you come to a wide, obvious path crossing the levada (ⓐ). It leads diagonally up from a house and electricity poles below on the left. Follow the path uphill to the right. The climb is gradual at first, through farmland; you are heading towards the saddle which can be seen above. Later brush and bilberry take over, leading to forests of mimosa and pine. The air is delicious and fresh, with just a hint of salt blowing in from the sea. Within **1h10min** you reach the lip of the coast at **Boca do Risco** (the 'dangerous gap'; ❶). Here are huge houseleeks, snowball trees, thistles, gorse, ferns, laurel, heath and wild flowers in every colour imaginable. Off across the sea to the northeast, Porto Santo may be clearly visible.

Turn left to make for Porto da Cruz on a path that will be quite narrow in places. As you progress, look back east for a view of the Ilhéu do Guincho

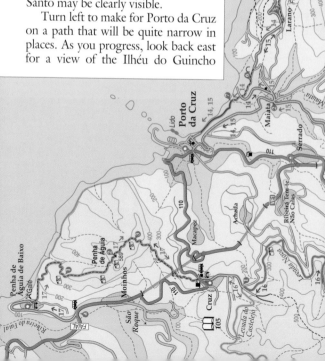

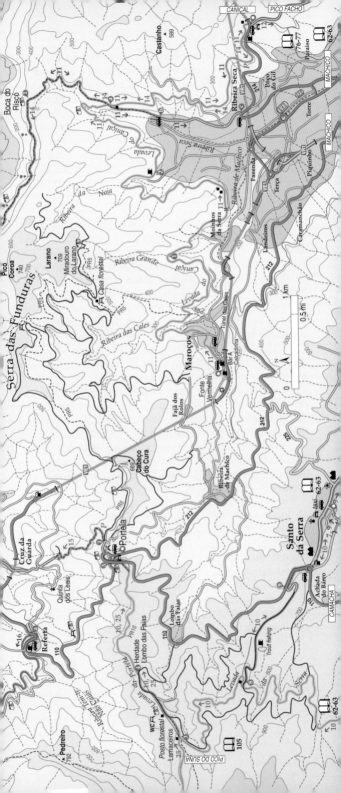

('Screech Islet') — so called because the wind shrieks through its tiny eyelet. This is one of our favourite views … dazzling in morning sun or glimmering in afternoon glow. Then new headlands come into view and, by **2h20min**, you'll reach a promontory with a stone marker ('JMG') just above the **Espigão Amarelo** ('Sharp Yellow Point'; ❷) … a splendid lunch spot. As you take a break here, you may be as awe-struck as we are by the fencing the shepherds have built below the path and down the cliffs. Even more baffling is the narrow strip of cultivated terraces in the east, stretching almost all the way from the cliff-top down to the sea on what looks like a 60° slope!

The character of the coastal path changes dramatically beyond the stone marker, its starkness soon softened by pine forests and, in the autumn, banks of pink belladonna lilies. You look down to a sea of palest turquoise through pine trees standing tall in ochre-red soil. The waves break over the rocks below again and again and again, creating endless patterns of the finest lace. Before long you catch your first views of Porto da Cruz, huddled below Eagle Rock. In the foreground, a dinosaur's back of a ridge thrusts out into the sea.

By this time a track (❸) and then a concrete road have come underfoot. You pass a GOODS HOIST on the right — and an INFORMATION BOARD for fitness trails in the northeast: notice the blue 'vertical' trail: it starts under 300m down the road, on the left. At **3h05min** the concrete road leaves the cliff. You descend into a valley with emerald crops and laden vines. Now either stay on the road, reaching asphalt in **Larano** (❺; **3h20min**) … or test your stamina on the FITNESS TRAIL (❹), which drops down steps on the left to a levada and then rises up more steps to Larano; you can see its whole length ahead.

From Larano follow the asphalt downhill, going right at the fork some 300m along. In 10 minutes, the road bends sharply left. Straight ahead you'll see a small hill with access doors to hillside storage caves. Leave the road here: descend concrete steps to the right. You pass to the left of the CAVES (❻) on a path beside a narrow levada and descend to a road. Cross over and turn right for 10-15m/yds, then go left down steps towards a two-wheel track visible on the shoreline. Cross the **Ribeira da Maiata** (❼; **3h40min**)* and follow the coast into **Porto da Cruz** (**4h**). The BUS STOP is uphill, on the main ER110, by the CENTRO DE SAUDE (◯).

---

*Should the river bed be flooded (only likely after a severe winter storm), you will have to follow the road above the river to the left for 500m/yds, back to the Larano road. Turn right here, then turn right on the road to Porto da Cruz (add 35-40 minutes). From the road there is a fine view of your destination, focusing on its rock, old sugar refinery and church.

Walk 15: FROM PORTELA TO PORTO DA CRUZ

Map pages 80-81	Distance: 5km/3mi; 1h55min

Grade: ● ‼ moderate descent of 600m/1970ft, of which 300m is very steep. You must be sure-footed. The trail is slippery in wet weather.

Equipment: walking boots, long trousers, sunhat, water, walking stick

How to get there: 🚐 53 or 78 to Portela
To return: 🚐 53 or 78 from Porto da Cruz

Alternative walk: Portela — Larano — Alternative walk 14. ● ‼ 11km/6.8mi; 4h40min. Grade, access as above. Follow the main walk until it turns down left to the river. Just 15m/yds *before* these steps, climb an old stone-laid path on the right past (**6**). Concrete steps take you up to a road: turn left to Larano (**5**; 2h) for Alternative walk 14 on page 79.

In the 1800s the *borracheiros* used this trail to transport wine, carried in goatskins on their backs, from Porto da Cruz to the south. Visually stunning in its own right, this walk is an ideal approach to Alternative walk 14.

Begin at **Portela**: from the bus stop on the ER212 (**0**) take steps up to the VIEWPOINT (**5**) on the higher ER110. Walk down this road, then fork left at the restaurant 'MIRA-DOURO DA PORTELA'. After 150m (**P**15) turn left on an old stone-laid trail (**1**; 'CAMINHO MUNICIPAL'). Zigzag steeply down, enjoying the superb view shown below. The trail becomes tarred and you meet a crossing road (**40min**). Turn right for 15m, then go sharp left down a minor road. Continue steeply down through the strung-out village of **Cruz da Guarda**.

When you reach a T-junction by the **Ribeira da Maiata** (**2**; **1h25min**), turn right, cross the BRIDGE, then take the first left turn. After 75m (just before a SCHOOL), turn left again. Descend this road for 500m along the east side of the river (if the river is in spate, see the footnote opposite!). Then take steps down left, cross the river (**7**) and follow the visible seaside track into **Porto da Cruz** (**1h55min**). The BUS STOP is uphill, on the main ER110, by the CENTRO DE SAUDE (**0**).

Strung-out villages straddle the ridges between Portela and Eagle Rock.

Walk 16: CRUZ • LEVADA DO CASTELEJO • CRUZ

Map pages 80-81, then 105   Distance: 11.6km/7.2mi; 2h50min
Grade: ● ‼ easy (ascent/descent of under 100m/330ft), but you must be sure-footed and have a head for heights (*danger of vertigo*). At the time of writing all the severe drops were well protected.
Equipment: walking boots, long trousers, sunhat, picnic, water
How to get there and return: 🚌 53 or 78 to/from Cruz, or 🚗: park beside the tiny electricity substation at Cruz, east of Faial (32° 46.264'N, 16° 50.614'W); there's a snack bar and separate bar opposite.
Alternative walk: Levada Nova — Levada do Castelejo — Cruz. ● ‼ 15km/9.3mi; 3h30min. Grade, equipment, return as above. 🚌 53 or 78 to the Achada turn-off ('ish-**trah**-dah pah-rah Ah-**shah**-dah'). From the bus stop, walk down the main road past the 'Referta' sign as far as the road to Cruz da Guarda on the right. Pick up the Levada Nova (ⓐ) here, below the road on the *left,* and follow its sluggish flow towards Penha de Águia, through the pretty, but extraordinarily named valley of Tem-te Não Caias ('Hold on; watch you don't fall!'). Some 50min along, you cross a narrow road and join the main walk at its 10min-point (❶).

Utter bliss! Following a narrow levada, in just over an hour you move from the cornucopia of cultivation below Penha de Águia into the wilderness of the Ribeiro Frio, with its limpid pools, mimosas and ancient fine-leaved laurels.

Start the walk at **Cruz** (**O**), a few paces uphill from the ELECTRICITY SUBSTATION. Almost opposite the 'Cruz' sign there are two *adjacent* roads: climb the road on the right (signpost: 'LEVADA DO CASTELEJO'), passing a bar/shop on your right immediately. At a Y-fork (**5min**), *keep left* (even if 'Levada do Castelejo' is signposted both left and right. Within **10min** you come to the **Levada do Castelejo** (❶), on your right. *(The Alternative walk comes in here, from the left.)* Turn right, walking against the current. Lime-green vines will frame your photographs of Penha de Águia, São Roque and Faial.

Beyond a road crossing (**20min**), you round a promontory and soon see Faial's church down to the right. São Roque's church, on the next *lombo,* seems close enough to touch. Then you turn sharp left up the magnificent valley of the **Ribeira de São Roque** (*P*16). In **40min** the levada channel is but a ribbon on the escarpment (❷), but steel railings and wires afford at least psychological protection. Other drops are encountered further on, but they are all protected, and the path is at least 60cm/2ft wide.

In **1h25min** you're at the levada's source; stone steps take you down to a dam in the boulder-strewn **Ribeiro Frio** (❸). The pools are so clear that you might be tempted to swim. Only birdsong disturbs the peace of this primeval place.

From here return to **Cruz** (**O**; **2h50min**).

Walks 16 and 17 look out over São Roque and across the Metade and Seca valleys to the high peaks.

Walk 17: PENHA DE ÁGUIA

Map pages 80-81   **Distance:** 3.3km/2mi; 2h30min

Grade: ● :: a strenuous climb of 450m/1475ft and descent of 350m/1150ft. The upward path is diabolically slippery, with grit, loose soil and pine needles underfoot. *Only recommended for very experienced walkers and only advisable in summer,* when local walkers will have hacked a way through the dense foliage. ***Danger of vertigo!***

Equipment: walking boots, sunhat, long-sleeved shirt, long trousers, picnic, water, whistle, walking stick; extra fleece and windproof in cool weather

How to get there: 🚌 53, 56 or 78 to Porto da Cruz, then 🚕 *taxi* to the Restaurante Galé in Penha de Águia de Baixo; or 🚗 to Penha de Águia de Baixo (the turn-off is just east of the São Roque River; Car tour 4); park near the Restaurante Galé (32° 47.295'N, 16° 50.837'W).
To return: 🚌 53 or 78 from Cruz — back to your base, or to the Penha de Águia de Baixo turn-off, from where you can walk back to your car (add 1.1km/20min).

Alternative ascent from Cruz: ● :: To climb and descend the same way, begin at Cruz (equipment/grade as above; ascent of 350m). 🚌 53 or 78 or 🚗 to Cruz (❶); park as for Walk 16 opposite. Some 15m below (east of) the sub-station (30m below the bus shelter), cross the road and walk up the lane on the right-hand side of the snack bar (*ignore* the signpost 'Vereda da Penha d'Águia' opposite the sign for the Levada do Castelejo). After just a few metres/yards, turn right in front of a house, on a narrow, sometimes overgrown path (just past the house there will be a narrow levada on your left). Your path up the mountain begins 230m/yds along; it rises steeply up steps on the left (*no* waymarking). Once on the top, (❸) climb left for 10 minutes to the trig point (❷). Return the same way.

W hen we first did this hike, we were torn to shreds by the most impenetrable jungle of lacerating ferns, gorse and blackberries we'd ever encountered. Although the path has been improved in recent years, the best tip is to tackle this walk in summer or early autumn, after the holiday season has started for the young Madeiran walkers. Unless they precede

you with their machetes, you may not even *find* the uphill path, let alone enjoy the views! Since this hike is only recommended for *very experienced walkers*, we have not described the zigs and zags in detail.

Start out at **Penha de Águia de Baixo** (◐): climb concrete steps between the RESTAURANTE GALÉ on the left and a house on the right. Immediately beyond the buildings, continue on the concreted walkway with street lights, crossing a small road. The walkway ends by the last house in the village, and the ascent begins in earnest. You stumble through blackberries and over broken stretches of path. Sometimes you will lose the path as it crosses bedrock. *Always keep an eye open for unexpected zigzags and aim for the 'dip' between the two 'summits' above.* The path climbs the right-hand side of a densely wooded ravine which opens out 300m/1000ft above the sea in a small waterfall (hidden from view).

In **55min** you reach the top of the rock's western ridge at a fork (❶): to the right are views down to the sea; ahead is an abyss. Go left, following the ridge and skirting the valley below on the left. Five minutes later you are just above the road to Penha de Águia de Baixo, and this is the best part of the walk. The path, coated with pine needles, is wide and almost level, and there are superb views below on the right, focusing on São Roque and the Metade and Seca valleys, with the high peaks as a backdrop.

Beyond this lovely 'user-friendly' section comes the most unpleasant part of the walk. Even if young Madeirans have hacked out the path for you, you will need all fours to haul yourself steeply up over broken tree roots. It seems never-ending, but you finally stagger up to the trig point at the top of **Penha de Águia** (❷; 589m/1930ft) in **1h30min**. Now, whenever you are on the north coast, you can look up to this tall white pillar and say with justifiable satisfaction: *I did it!*

Continue along the lip of the mountainside, past the pillar. In seven minutes you come to a SADDLE (❸; 550m/1800ft) and a rock outcrop on the right. The path descending from here is usually in better condition than the ascent route, but still demands your full attention. Zigzag down, sometimes through pines, for about 50 minutes. You eventually drop down to a narrow levada; turn right along it. On coming to houses, turn left down to the ER110 at **Cruz** (◐; **2h30min**), where you will find a three watering holes. The Funchal bus stops at a BUS SHELTER a few steps uphill to the right on the far side of the road. But if you have left your car at the start of the walk, catch a Faial-bound bus opposite the shelter and ask the conductor for '**Pain**-yah day **Ah**-gee-ah, Rish-toh-**rahnt** Gah-**lay**'. Alight at the BRIDGE (❹) over the São Roque River and climb the road back to your car (add 20 minutes).

Walk 18: SANTANA • SÃO JORGE • VIGIA

Photograph page 28   Distance: 9.5km/6mi; 3h30min

Grade: ● ‡ moderate-strenuous, with over 400m/1300ft of descents and corresponding ascents; *possibility of vertigo. Not recommended in damp weather, when the trails would be slippery, or in strong winds.*

Equipment: walking boots, raingear, windproof, fleece, long trousers, swimwear, sunhat, picnic, water

How to get there: 🚐 103 or 138 (Arco bus); ask for '**Vail**-yoh So-**lahr**' (the old *solar*); the stop is 1.7km northwest of Santana's town hall — its official name is 'Pico Tanoeiro'. By 🚗: park in São Jorge (32°49.596'N, 16°54.398'W) and take 🚐 103 or 138 to the start.
To return: 🚐 103 from the Vigia turn-off at São Jorge, back to base or back to your car; *be there at least 10min before departure time from São Jorge.*

Shorter walk: Santana — São Jorge. ● ‡ 7km/4.3mi; 2h37min. Grade/ equipment/access/return as above. End the walk at São Jorge (❼).

An old zigzag trail, high cliffs, the throbbing sea beside you ... this walk was made in heaven. And if you're heartbroken when it ends, you'll be happy to know that some other sections of old cobbled trail still exist — see the 'Appetizer', Walk 3, Alternative walk 25-1, Walk 27b or Walk 40.

Start out from the 'PICO TANOEIRO' BUS STOP (◉): walk back 20m or so towards Funchal, then turn left up a lane. In **4min** you come to the remains of a rosy-pink *solar,* one of the island's early manors. Leave the lane by cutting right in front of the façade, curving below the building on a track (initially concreted), overlooking the **Achada do Gramacho**, a small plain laced with vines. Meet the lane again, cross it, and on reaching the QUINTA DO FURÃO, turn right beside the car park on your left. Follow signs to 'VIEWPOINT/VINEYARDS' just past the pub (❶), to where fencing guides you round the north side of the hotel and a conical hill, the **Cabeço da Vigia**. When the fencing ends, keep along the edge of the cliffs on a narrow path. As the path dives down right, take steps up left to a turning circle. Follow the road ahead for 130m, then turn sharp right down an earthen track (❷; sign: 'SÃO JORGE, CALHAU').

Soon the old cobbled trail can be seen beneath the iron-rich soil. You've begun the exhilarating descent into the **Ribeira de São Jorge**. The setting is magnificent: the great peaks rise inland while, ahead of you, São Jorge's church and lighthouse shimmer brightly above a blue, blue sea. On the far side of the valley, you can see your old cobbled trail up to São Jorge. Another path skirts the coast.

All too soon the descent ends; at **1h** you skirt to the left of a cheerful bar/restaurant and lido, then cross an old bridge over the river. Turn right and follow the coastal path past a well-kept house on the left, then one on the right. The rest of **Calhau** (❸) is in ruins, but this was once such an important port that it boasted both a church *and* a chapel! Opposite the first of the ruins on the right is a tap and the trail we'll climb

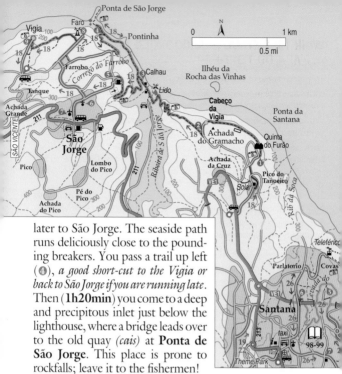

later to São Jorge. The seaside path runs deliciously close to the pounding breakers. You pass a trail up left (❹), *a good short-cut to the Vigia or back to São Jorge if you are running late*. Then (**1h20min**) you come to a deep and precipitous inlet just below the lighthouse, where a bridge leads over to the old quay *(cais)* at **Ponta de São Jorge**. This place is prone to rockfalls; leave it to the fishermen!

Return to Calhau (❸; **1h40min**), then turn up the steep trail by the tap. As you climb, look across to your descending trail, etched into the cliff opposite. By **2h15min** you will have huffed and puffed up to a road junction with a CAFÉ (❺) to the left. Follow the road almost straight ahead (the RUA DE SÃO PEDRO, the third road from the right), rising past the gates of a CEMETERY (**2h25min**). After seven minutes you skirt a tiny CHAPEL (❻) on the left. Continue round left to the magnificent baroque CHURCH at **São Jorge** (❼; **2h37min**). Nearby are a BAR and a BUS STOP. *(The Shorter walk ends here.)*

Walk back to the chapel (❻) and turn left. Ignore a road off right; continue ahead along the ESTRADA MUNICIPAL DO FARROBO. Beyond a stream (**Corrego do Farrobo**), rise to a T-junction and turn right to the LIGHTHOUSE (❽; **3h**). Walk back from the lighthouse 80m/yds, then turn right on a concrete walkway (red lettering 'Vigia'; arrow). When the concrete ends, follow a red earthen track past a track and then steps on the left. At a Y-fork go right; the track becomes a path and curls left. You are aiming for the circular white building up ahead. At a T-junction, turn right to a road. Turn right again, to the **Vigia** ('look-out', once used by whalers; ❾; **3h25min**). From here you look out over Ponta Delgada's seaside church and hotel, with Cabanas above, to Ribeira da Janela in the distance. Take the road back out to the Estrada Municipal do Farrobo (❿; **3h30min**), to flag down a bus at the 'VIGIA' sign.

Walk 19: PICO DO ARIEIRO • PICO RUIVO • ACHADA DO TEIXEIRA

Map on reverse of touring map; more photos on pages 4 , 93, cover

Distance: 8.6km/5.3mi; 3h40min

Grade: ● ‼ very strenuous, with steep ascents (about 500m/1650ft) and descents (about 750m/2450ft) overall. You must be sure-footed and have a head for heights (***danger of vertigo***). Five tunnels en route (20min total). ***Sometimes impassable due to landslides or snowfall.*** Partly Route PR1

Equipment: walking boots, raingear, windproof, fleece, long trousers, whistle, sunhat, picnic, plastic bottle/water purifying tablets, torch, walking stick(s)

How to get there and return: 🚕 *taxi* to Pico do Arieiro and back from the Achada do Teixeira (or with friends who are touring; Car tour 4)

Short walk: Pico do Arieiro — first or second viewpoint — Pico do Arieiro. ● ‼ 35min-1h15min. Stout shoes, sunhat. Ups and downs on hundreds of steps; you must be sure-footed and fairly agile; *possibility of vertigo*. Access: 🚕 car or *taxi* to Pico do Arieiro (32°44.100'N, 16°55.717'W).

Alternative walks

1 **Pico do Arieiro — Pico Ruivo via the Torres.** ● ‼ 10.5km/6.5mi; 4h45min. Grade as above (ascents about 650m/2130ft, descents 800m/2620ft). One 100m-long tunnel. This is the main route from Arieiro to Ruivo (PR1), but has been closed for several years due to rockfall. It is even more strenuous than the tunnel route. Follow the main walk through Pico do Gato (45min), then fork right (③). After a short downward stretch, the *real* climbing begins, over hundreds of steps. It takes a good 45 minutes to reach the pass on the eastern shoulder of the Torres (●; 1800m/5900ft; 1h30min). Beyond the pass, the path curves left and zigzags down more steps (there are also some skiddy scree sections). Finally (2h20min) you come to a junction: the original trail, to the right, is broken (dotted red line on our map). The sixth (final) tunnel of the original westerly route is on your left. Go through it and pick up the text below at (④; 1h15min-point), to take the westerly detour trail to Ruivo.

2 **Pico do Arieiro — Pico Ruivo — Queimadas — Santana.** ● ‼ 16km/10mi; 6h. *Only suitable after a long period of dry weather.* Equipment and access as main walk; add another 1200m/3900ft of steep descent. Only for masochistic experts! Do the main walk, then cross the car park at the Achada. Go to the front of the building and walk past it. Below is the basaltic dyke shown on page 93, Homem em Pé (④). Descend to the right of it and continue down to the road not far below. Cross the road: the path continues at the left of the roadside viewpoint. *From here on the very steep clay path can be as slippery as ice.* Some 1h20min from the Achada, go through a gate and soon reach the upper house in the story-book setting of Queimadas Park. From the lower house (1h30min) take the steep road down towards Santana. Once level with the theme park, cut right on Rua do Til to reach the main road. Buses 56, 103 and 138 all leave from opposite the Health Centre, where you emerge.

3 **Pico do Arieiro — Pico Ruivo — Torrinhas — Curral.** ● ‼ 14.6km/9mi; 6h15min. Add 1000m/3300ft of steep descent. Do the main walk and, at Pico Ruivo, pick up Alternative walk 20 on page 92.

T ry to make a *very* early morning start and get to Pico do Arieiro at daybreak. The sun erupts like a ball of fire; shards of light cascade mauve and golden over mountaintops and valleys. The mists clear quickly but reluctantly, curling

*Do start out early! This photograph was taken at about 10.30, just below Pico do Arieiro. The mists are already descending, obscuring the first viewpoint (to the right) and the Torres peaks behind it. Pico do Cidrão is the attractive red wedge on the left, at the head of the Cidrão and Metade ravines. Built in the late 1960s, Madeira's most famous mountain trail is very well engineered, and the difficult stretches are protected by sturdy fencing. The fences sometimes come down in storms — or landslides block the tunnels — but this route is so popular that repairs are made fairly quickly (always check for path closures as explained on page 36). If you are unlucky enough to walk just after rockfall, **please use good judgement and turn back.***

lovingly around the peaks, mere wisps and whispers and then they're gone. A shepherd appears suddenly from beneath a crest, shouldering a heavy load of firewood, sending goats and sheep scurrying between light and shade, as fluffy clouds throw shadows across the scrubby slopes.

The photograph on page 119 gives you a good overview of your route. Here on **Pico do Arieiro** (⊙), Madeira's third highest peak (1818m/5965ft), you are far above the great Cidrão and Metade ravines. **Start the walk** behind the restaurant just below the summit: a sign indicates 'PR1 PICO RUIVO E 7KM' ('E' meaning 'este', east) and 'PICO RUIVO O 5.6KM' ('O' for 'oeste', west). In fact the routes are identical *except* that halfway along the westerly route uses tunnels below the Pico das Torres, while the easterly route goes mainly over the peak (Alternative walk 1). *Both* routes were damaged in 2014; this description was valid at press date, but may change.

Follow the paved path shown above. You cross a very narrow spine — a foretaste of the great chasms to follow on this trail linking the island's three highest mountains. The ups and downs begin almost at once, as you struggle over a massive knoll protruding from the spine and then descend to a grassy verge (*P*19), a fine picnic spot. At a T-junction, turn right to the first viewpoint, the **Miradouro Ninho da Manta** (Buzzard's Nest; ❶; **15min**), from where there is a good view down to Fajã da Nogueira, setting for Walk 24. From here you can also see the path climbing the eastern flanks of the **Torres**, the island's second highest mountain. The jagged

90

teeth crowning this 'Peak of the Towers' hide Ruivo from view for most of the walk. But you *can* see the island's highest peak — and, on a clear day, the outskirts of Funchal — from the second viewpoint (with rock-hewn picnic table; **25min**).

In **30min** a steep descent on yet more steps begins; at the bottom, a ROCK ARCH will frame your photographs. Go through the arch and soon look right for splendid views over the Metade Valley and the village of São Roque on its *lombo*.

A FIRST TUNNEL (**2**) is met in **45min**; it passes through the isolated needle of **Pico do Gato** ('Cat's Peak'). At the exit, keep *left* at the FORK (**3**), unless a sign warns that the route ahead is closed. Go on into the SECOND TUNNEL (**1h**); the THIRD, FOURTH AND FIFTH TUNNELS follow quickly. Just past the fifth tunnel, the longer easterly route joins you at a signposted junction (**4**; **1h15min**). It has emerged from what was once the sixth tunnel on this westerly route which crossed the spine; the path to the east has collapsed. At this point *both* trails make a long detour to the west, climbing over the ridge on a series of metal ladders/steps secured to the rock face.

Once over the PASS (**2h**), you can see where the old path (red dots on our map) has fallen off the cliff on the right. Soon you have sweeping vistas over the Metade; spikes of burnt heath trees rise above the regenerating greenery. It's a tiring slog up to the Ruivo REST HOUSE (**a**; **2h30min**), where you should be able to buy refreshments. After tackling the SUMMIT OF **Pico Ruivo** (**b**; **2h40min**), follow the paved PATH from the rest house down to **Achada do Teixeira** (**c**; **3h40min**).

Walk 20: ACHADA DO TEIXEIRA • PICO RUIVO • TORRINHAS • ENCUMEADA

Map on reverse of touring map   **Distance:** 13km/8mi; 6h25min

Grade: ● ❘❘ very strenuous, with overall ascents of 550m/1800ft and descents of 1100m/3600ft. Red/yellow waymarking (PR1.2, then PR1.3). You must be sure-footed and have a head for heights (*danger of vertigo*). *Avoid the walk in wet weather, when the hundreds of stone steps are slippery.* Expect to be caught up in mists. We have never encountered landslides en route, but don't discount the possibility. You must walk quickly, too; bus times are very tight! *Important note:* Several paths radiate north and south from this walk, but only the PR2 route between Curral and Boaventura (part of which is covered in the Alternative walk below) is used regularly. *Experts* may wish to tackle some of the others — which we mention in passing — but we can not recommend any of them.

Equipment: walking boots, raingear, windproof, fleece, long trousers, whistle, compass, sunhat, picnic, plastic bottle/water purifying tablets, walking stick

How to get there: 🚌 56, 103 or 138 to Santana or 🚌 53, 56, 78 or 103 to Faial, then 🚕 *taxi* to the Achada do Teixeira. You will have to walk faster than our times to catch 🚌 6! Consider staying overnight in Santana, to give you time to *savour* this walk; you might even start at sunrise, as we do (arrange this with a taxi in advance).
To return: 🚌 6 from Encumeada (or telephone from the bar at Encumeada for a Ribeira Brava taxi and take a later bus from Ribeira Brava).

Short walk: Achada do Teixeira — Pico Ruivo — Achada do Teixeira. ● 5.5km/3.4mi; 1h50min. Moderate climb/descent of 270m/900ft on a stone-paved path (PR1.2; shelters, springs en route). Stout shoes, fleece, windproof, sunhat, picnic, water. Access: as above (ask the taxi to wait or to return for you), or by 🚕 (32° 45.900'N, 16° 55.257'W; Car tour 4).

Alternative walk: Achada do Teixeira — Pico Ruivo — Torrinhas — Curral. ● ❘❘ 10.6km/6.6mi; 5h30min. Access, equipment, grade as above (but a further 400m/1300ft of very steep descent, mostly on a path through shady eucalyptus. From Torrinhas Pass (**❸**), descend the PR2 (red/yellow flashes). You reach the bridge over the Ribeira do Curral 1h45min below Torrinhas, at Fajã dos Cardos (**❹**; just under 5h), where you can catch 🚌 81 just above or below where the walk emerges — or you could climb up to Fajã Escura (**ⓑ**), Colmeal (**ⓒ**) or Curral (**○**; 6h).

B lood red, then mauve; and finally silver and blue and gold. All was shadow; all was light. Nothing was real. Where sky ended and sea began, where mountains soared and clouds tiptoed down — all was merged into one. Sunrise at Pico Ruivo, the ideal time to start this walk.
   Start out at the **Achada do Teixeira** (**○**; *P*20). First walk behind the house to admire the view shown opposite (**ⓓ**), then head west on the paved ridge path to Pico Ruivo (sign: 'PR1.2, 2.8km'). You'll pass some springs and shelters on the way and enjoy wonderful views of Arieiro, the Torres and the path of Walk 19 (**40min**). This path from Arieiro comes in from the left, and you quickly reach the government REST HOUSE below Pico Ruivo (**ⓐ**; **45min**; refreshments usually available).
   Five minutes above the house, you'll come to a saddle and a PR1 sign (5.1km from here to Torrinhas Pass and 11.2km

to Encumeada). At the left are steps to the SUMMIT of **Pico Ruivo** (ⓑ; 1862m/6105ft; **55min**), with its viewpoints. You'll want to linger up here to see how many landmarks you can spot, including the Pico das Torres, Torrinhas Pass, Pico Grande, the Paúl da Serra, the Metade and Curral valleys, and the *pousadas* at Queimadas. To the northeast Porto Santo floats like a cloud on the horizon.

From the summit, return to the sign and turn down left for Encumeada. As the well-waymarked path descends the northwestern flanks of Ruivo, take the opportunity to climb up slightly to the right, to see the fantastic views over the north coast, about 1300m/4250ft below. Twenty minutes below the saddle, the valley leading down to Curral das Freiras opens up before you almost at once, and you can see the higher hamlet of Fajã dos Cardos (on the route of the Alternative walk).

In **1h40min** come to a particularly good viewpoint over Curral's setting; now the path dips down south for a while, before resuming its westerly course. In **1h55min** start climbing to skirt a cone-shaped sandstone peak on your right ... all the while enjoying the perfume of wild oregano and thyme crushed underfoot.

At **2h05min** you'll reach a promontory with chasms to the left. Fifteen minutes later a path, indicated on a rock, heads up right, before descending to São Jorge via Pico Canário (❶; **2h20min**). At **2h25min** climb down some steps and into another valley, from where you can again see the north coast. Already you can see across the great valleys of the Ribeira Brava and São Vicente rivers, which split the island in two, and the pronounced hairpins of the road from Miradouro (Walk 29) to the Paúl da Serra.

Homem em Pé ('Man on Foot'), an impressive basaltic dyke just below the Achada do Teixeira house. From here there is a fine view down over the São Jorge Valley (Picnic 20; Alternative walk 19-1).

In **2h45min**, find a perfect promontory for lunch. Here two or three people can sit wedged in nature's rock-chairs and picnic overlooking Curral das Freiras. This is just after a fork where a path descends left to Curral, but this is *not* the path we recommend for the Alternative walk. We go *right* here. The most hazardous section of the walk is soon encountered: back on the north side of the ridge, the path descends about a dozen steep and SLIPPERY STONE STEPS BESIDE A PRECIPICE (➋). There are good protective railings here, but they sometimes come down in storms, so if they are not in place *stow everything away before you make this potentially dangerous descent.* And watch your footing on the very slippery section that follows. Then — accompanied by the aroma of wild mint — reach a grassy verge overlooking the north coast — an ideal picnic spot for groups of walkers.

Soon you are confronted by the first of *many* flights of steep stone steps. These lead up to **Torrinhas Pass** (➌; **3h**), where signs point the way to Curral, Pico Ruivo, and Encumeada. *(The Alternative route descends to the left here.)* There is also a sign for the Vereda do Urzal, the newly-cleared PR2 trail north to Lombo do Urzal and Boaventura (although its lower reaches have succumbed to the asphalt of the ER220 and ER211). The path now takes you over the shoulders of **Pico do Jorge** (➍) — forever up and forever down — a climb and descent of over 200m/650ft lasting almost an hour, on giant-sized steps.

You come to a first a SPRING on the left (**4h30min**), and enjoy lovely views of the valleys of Serra de Água and São Vicente. Then you descend through a glen of giant ferns beside a basalt escarpment at **Pico do Ferreiro** (➎). At **4h55min** you may see a steep path down left: it is part of a 1800s trail to the Jardim da Serra via Pico Grande. We know a couple of *experts* who have walked it, but we have *not*. Another SPRING is passed, this one signposted (**5h20min**).

This part of the walk, west of Pico do Jorge, can be glorious. But mists frequently descend by early afternoon, obscuring the valleys. Mist will be a boon for those who suffer from vertigo: the hundreds *and hundreds* of STONE STEPS on which you descend 300m/1000ft to the end of the walk seem to spiral in space, but in heavy mist the abyss is not apparent, and all you can see are the many nearby *folhados* (wild lily of the valley trees). Fortunately the steps are amply wide!

Eventually a steep dirt track takes you to the ER228 at **Encumeada** (◉; 1004m/3293ft; **6h25min**). Walk 31 can begin here, at the *miradouro* over the São Vicente Valley. Follow the road south over the pass, to find the SIGN TO FOLHADAL beside the **Levada do Norte**, starting point for Walk 32. Wait here for the BUS, or telephone for a taxi from the bar.

Walk 21: PICO DAS PEDRAS • COVA DA RODA • CRUZINHAS

Map pages 98-99   **Distance:** 7.2km/4.5mi; 2h35min

Grade: ● easy-moderate ups and downs, with a descent of 600m/1950ft, and an ascent of 180m/590ft at the end of the walk

Equipment: stout shoes (walking boots preferable), long trousers, windproof, sunhat, fleece, picnic, water

How to get there: 🚌 53, 56 or 78 to Faial or 🚌 56, 103 or 138 to Faial or Santana, then 🚕 *taxi* to Pico das Pedras on the ER218
To return: 🚌 56, 103 or 138 from Cruzinhas

Short walk: ● Pico das Pedras — Queimadas — Pico das Pedras. 4km/2.5mi; 1h10min. This very wide trail (officially called a 'walk for everyone') is easy, *but* wear lace-up shoes with good grip (the path can be *very* slippery); take picnic, water. Access: 🚕 car or *taxi* to/from Pico das Pedras (●), where the Levada do Caldeirão Verde crosses the ER218 road (32° 46.771'N, 16° 53.726'W; Car tour 4). Walk through the small holiday complex, with the chalets to the left: the levada continues on the far side of the buildings; follow it to Queimadas (●) and back.

Alternative walk: Queimadas — Caldeirão Verde — Cruzinhas. ● ⁞⁞ 19.8km/12.3mi; 6h30min. Grade, equipment, access: see Walk 22, page 97. Do Walk 22 first. On returning to Queimadas from Caldeirão Verde, follow the levada to the crossing of the ER218 at Pico das Pedras. Then do the walk described below. Return on 🚌 56 or 103 from Cruzinhas.

T his walk is at its best in summer or early autumn, when the hydrangeas bordering the levada are bursting with melon-sized blossoms and the tiny terraces in the valleys are aglow with golden hayricks.

Start the walk at **Pico das Pedras** (●), with its 'Santana' cottages. The **Levada do Caldeirão Verde** crosses the ER218 here. Follow the blue and yellow sign, heading southeast for 'FAIAL' (or, for the Short walk, go west towards 'QUEIMADAS'). Stroll beside the levada under the shade of holm oaks, eucalyptus and a 'forest' of cornflower-blue hydrangeas. After **10min** turn left down a track, with the levada beside you on your left. Five minutes later, turn down left again; don't follow the narrow levada ahead — the path is too over-

Hydrangeas flank the start of the walk, near Pico das Pedras

The steep terracing in the Ribeira Seca near Cruzinhas is at its most colourful in summer.

grown. Some **20min** along, cross straight over a track. Further on, ignore a track turning back to the right. Keep ahead downhill to a crossroads with a tree in the middle, facing a house (**❶**; **35min**). This is **Cova da Roda**. A track goes left to Santana, and the one we have been descending continues ahead as a tarred road through market gardens, also to Santana. Turn down *sharp right* here (the 'CRUZINHAS' sign was missing at press date).

As you descend this earthen track, look out for an over-grown grassy track on your left 300m/yds along. (If you miss it, your earthen track will end at a waterhouse by a tunnel bored for water exploration; just retrace your steps for under 200m to find the grassy track, on your *right*.) You descend to a STONE BRIDGE over the **Ribeira da Abelheira** (**❷**; **45min**) and rise up an old stone-laid trail on the far side. At a FORK (**❸**) 400m/yds past the bridge, turn left downhill. You soon have splendid views of 'Eagle Rock', before dropping down into the Lombo do Galego Valley.

At **Lombo Galego** (**❹**; **1h15min**) you meet a crossing road; follow it down to the *right* (despite a sign pointing left to 'Cruzinhas'! Left goes to *Faial*). The old trail has been preserved where possible; green and white signs 'VEREDA …' or 'CAMINHO …' mark the steps where it leaves the road. Keep watching for the old trail (easily identified by its street lights), to avoid the road. (But the road is so little used, and the beauty of the Ribeira Seca terracing so absorbing, that you may prefer just to follow the road!)

At **Fajã da Murta** you cross the **Ribeira Seca** (**❺**; **2h05min**), one of the three great rivers flowing to Faial. From here it's a 30-minute climb on the trail; you cross the road once more before reaching **Cruzinhas** and the ER103 (**❻**; **2h35min**). There is a large BUS SHELTER at the left.

Walk 22: QUEIMADAS • LEVADA DO CALDEIRÃO VERDE • SANTANA

Distance: 16.7km/10.4mi; 5h15min

Grade: ● ** moderate, but you must be sure-footed and have a head for heights. The levada path (PR9) is very slippery and broken away in places. *Danger of vertigo* throughout (very severe drops on one side, adequately protected by fences, *but these often come down in storms*). Four tunnels (10min total). Steep descent to Santana.

Equipment: walking boots, torch, long trousers, fleece, windproof, whistle, picnic, plastic bottle/water purifying tablets, walking stick

How to get there and return: 🚌 56, 103 or 138 or 🚗 to/from Santana (32° 48.275'N, 16° 52.898'W), then 🚕 *taxi* to Queimadas to begin the walk.

Short walks: Levada do Caldeirão Verde. ● ** Follow the main walk as long as you like; return the same way. Or follow the levada east to Pico das Pedras (● Short walk 21 in reverse). Take a picnic and fleece, and *wear lace-up shoes with very good grip; when damp, the red clay soil here is like a skating rink!* Be sure to ask the taxi driver to return for you. 🚗: Travelling by car, see the notes for Car tour 4 on pages 27-28: you may prefer to park at Pico das Pedras on the ER218 (see page 95).

Think green. Think of rain forests … of emeralds. This is Queimadas — a mossy paradise. Take advantage of the 10-minute break in the bus journey at Poiso or Ribeiro Frio and fortify yourself with a warm drink or a 'Madeiran breakfast' (a glass of sweet Madeira wine and a warm hard-boiled egg). This will set you up for the drop in temperature on the descent to the north coast — where as much as 2m/80in of rain can fall in a year!

When you arrive at **Queimadas Park** (○; *P*22), you will find two charming *pousadas*. **Begin the walk** by passing the lower houses, to discover yet another *pousada* — this one a miniature for the muscovy ducks who live in the pools. Cross the wooden bridge and follow the wide path beside the old

The fairytale setting of Queimadas (Walks 22, 23 and 28). Heath tree branches are used all over Madeira for fencing. Their gnarled curves make a pretty picture, straight out of a story book.

Levada do Caldeirão Verde. The red clay path can be *diabolically slippery* if damp, so take care. In **13min** pass through a gateway, beyond which the path narrows. Four minutes later, be sure to leave the levada where it is broken away.

The views are spectacular as you follow the levada westwards to one of the most remote parts of the island. After crossing two ravines — the **Ribeira dos Cedros (27min)** and the **Ribeira da Fonte do Louro (45min)** — you come in about **1h** to the first, very short TUNNEL. Two minutes beyond the exit, ignore the signposted PR1.1 path (❶) off right. *(Walk 28 leaves us here.)* Immediately you plunge into the second tunnel (five minutes). There is a path on the right at this tunnel exit, too; it joins the Ilha path. The third tunnel lies just beyond this path; it's very low: *keep your head down* for the next two minutes. Not far past this third tunnel, you must leave the levada again to avoid an overhanging precipice.

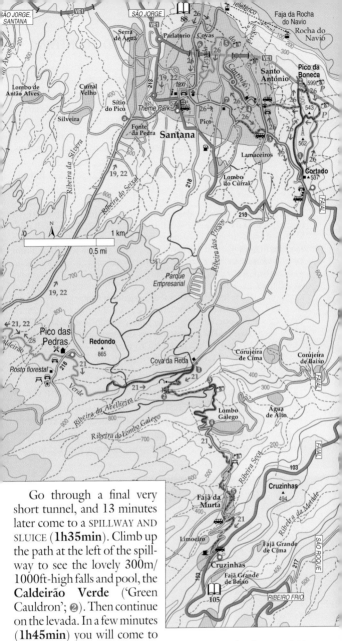

Go through a final very short tunnel, and 13 minutes later come to a SPILLWAY AND SLUICE (**1h35min**). Climb up the path at the left of the spillway to see the lovely 300m/ 1000ft-high falls and pool, the **Caldeirão Verde** ('Green Cauldron'; ❷). Then continue on the levada. In a few minutes (**1h45min**) you will come to our favourite picnic spot — a PROMONTORY in the sun (❸) overlooking the **Ribeira Grande**, 500m/1650ft below.

From here allow 3h30min to descend to **Santana** via the Queimadas road. Once level with the THEME PARK, cut right on RUA DO TIL (❹). This emerges opposite the HEALTH CENTRE on the main road (❺; **5h15min**), for buses 56, 103 and 138.

Walk 23: QUEIMADAS • CALDEIRÃO DO INFERNO • QUEIMADAS

Map pages 98-99 **Distance:** 15.5km/9.6mi; just over 5h

Grade: ● ‡‡ as Walk 22, page 97. This extension of the Caldeirão Verde walk, which used to be only suitable for experts, has recently been upgraded, with excellent protective fences. It's now the PR9 throughout.

Equipment: walking boots, long trousers, plastic rainhat, fleece, windproof, raingear, whistle, picnic, plastic bottle/water purifying tablets, torch, walking stick

How to get there and return: 🚐: see Walk 22, page 97, and add 1h30min to walk down to Santana. Or 🚗 car or *taxi* to/from Queimadas (32° 47.023'N, 16° 54.350'W) or Pico das Pedras (see page 95).

Alternative walk: Queimadas — Caldeirão do Inferno — Pico Ruivo tunnel — Fajã da Nogueira — ER103. ● ‡‡ 20km/12.4mi; 6h40min. Map continues on reverse of touring map. Grade, equipment, bus or taxi access as main walk. You will have to pass through a tunnel 2.4km/1.5mi long. *Each member of the party must carry a good torch.* Follow the main walk to the Caldeirão do Inferno. Then return to the Pico Ruivo tunnel (❹). Plunge in. You exit about 40min later by booming waterfalls and clear pools, where the Ribeira Seca, coming down from its source on the Pico das Torres, crashes into the levada (ⓐ). Another tunnel (ⓑ; 12min) lurks beyond this one. After these, the final few tunnels are a doddle. The levada is soon covered by a jeep track. About 1h30min from entering the Ruivo tunnel take the track down left to the power station (1h; Walk 24b ascends this track). From the power station walk on for 1h15min to the ER103 (🚐 56, 103) and *flag down a bus* on a straight stretch of road.

The awe-inspiring chasm of the Caldeirão do Inferno is hidden below the eastern flanks of Pico Canário and the northern escarpment of Ruivo — about as close to the heart of primeval Madeira as you can get. As always, the levada builders have been there before you, taming the wilderness and opening your path.

Water for the Levada dos Tornos is captured at three main sources (described in Walk 24, page 102); the Caldeirão do Inferno is just one of them. Left: crossing the Ribeira Grande, on the approach to the 'Inferno' ('Hell's Cauldron'). Right: at the source. Don't expect to see roaring waterfalls here; this is just surface water, pouring down from Pico Canário (1591m/5220ft). What is magnificent is the escarpment rising 300m/ 1000ft above you — at its most impressive after rain.

The walk begins at **Queimadas**. Use the notes for Walk 22, page 97, as far as the sunny promontory (❸; **1h45min**), then continue along the levada. Another impassable section of levada is met in **2h**: a stepped path down to the right takes you round it. In **2h05min** you come to STEPS up to the left (the Levada do Caldeirão Verde takes its source not far ahead, in a beautiful setting with a waterfall). These steps are easily climbed, but coming down it's another story — a descent into nothingness…

You ascend 80m/260ft to a newer levada, the **Levada do Pico Ruivo**, at 960m/3150ft (❹; **2h13min**). Two tunnels are seen ahead here. To the left is a short tunnel (no torch needed) opening onto more fine views. The 2.4km/1.5mi-long Pico Ruivo tunnel has old railway tracks dating from its excavation. Steps also continue uphill here, leading to a huge levada-workers' barbecue. To the right is a large WATER TANK. Skirt the edge of the tank (there is cable fencing). Just beyond the tank you have to walk under a waterfall and will no doubt get soaked.

Immediately afterwards, go through a first short TUNNEL. Three more follow. Then you come to roaring waterfalls in a cavern at the head of the **Ribeira Grande** (**2h27min**). This chasm is crossed via two very NARROW BRIDGES. There were sturdy metal handrails in place at press date, but these often come down in storms (as in the photograph opposite). Or, in dry weather, you can descend to the river bed. Beyond here you pass through four more short tunnels (if the first one *appears* to be blocked off, note that the opening is just a narrow gap at the right-hand side). You come to the setting shown below — the 300m/1000ft-high wall of the **Caldeirão do Inferno**   (**2h32min**),

source of the Levada do Pico Ruivo.

Dwarfed by this escarpment lies a tiny levada channel — just a trickle in a grassy sun-trap. It's so still you can almost hear the trees breathing. Relax at this magnificent picnic spot before returning to **Queimadas** (❶; just over **5h**) … or going on to the nearby valley of Fajã da Nogueira via the Pico Ruivo tunnel (❹; Alternative walk).

Walk 24: FAJÃ DA NOGUEIRA

Map: reverse of touring map   **Distance:** see Walks a and b below

Grade: ● both suggestions are easy-moderate, with a climb/descent of 400m/1300ft on tracks. (The initial climb on a jeep track is fairly tedious, but you will find it well worth the effort!)

Equipment: stout shoes, long trousers, sunhat, fleece, windproof, picnic, water, torch, walking stick

How to get there and return: 🚗 car (preferably jeep) or *jeep-taxi* to the power station at Fajã da Nogueira (32° 44.611'N, 16° 54.353'W), reached by a *very rough* dirt track. (Also accessible by 🚌 103 or 138 to the turn-off for the power station on the ER103; add 4.5km *each way*.)

Walk a: Pico da Nogueira. 9km/5.6mi; 2h30min. **Walk b: Ribeira Seca.** 9.6km/6mi; 3h40min. These routes diverge at the 40min-point.

Alternative walk: Levada do Pico Ruivo and Levada da Serra. ● ‼ 14.8km/9.2mi; 5h45min. *A more satisfying walk than either a or b above, but only recommended for sure-footed walkers with a head for heights (**danger of vertigo**).* At time of writing this path was adequately protected by cable fencing, but it often comes down in storms. Equipment as above, but wear walking boots; take a whistle and plastic bottle/water purifying tablets. Follow Walk b to the Ribeira Seca and back to (④). Continue *past* the track you ascended. Walk with the flow of the Levada do Pico Ruivo (and later the Levada da Serra) for 1h25min, until you come to a tunnel (🌫; 4h). Just inside it is the underground water tank (it was not possible to build this large reservoir on the open mountainside). Descend the track in front of the tunnel and, less than 10min downhill (just before a keepers' house), turn right uphill at a T-junction (②). You reach the top of the pipe on Pico da Nogueira, outside the tank (③; 35min from the tunnel). To return to the power station, go down the track and, at the fork before the keepers' house (②), continue down the main track. In 15min (5h) cross the Ribeira da Fajã da Nogueira. You meet your outgoing track 10min later (at ①), just above the clearing with the enormous *til* trees. The power station (◎) is 35min downhill.

The Levada dos Tornos (Walk 7) was born here in the wilderness of Fajã da Nogueira in 1971, when the power station was inaugurated. Water for the Tornos is captured at three main sources. One lies far to the northwest: an extremely long tunnel carries water from the Porco and São Jorge rivers directly to this power station. Another conduit is the rebuilt

Levada da Serra do Faial e Juncal, which runs from the Juncal River to an underground reservoir and then a pipe on Pico da Nogueira. The third source is the Caldeirão do Inferno (Walk 23): its waters flow through the Pico Ruivo tunnel to the same pipe, whence both levadas plummet down to the power station.

All the walks begin at **Fajã da Nogueira** (). Climb the jeep track at the right of the POWER STATION. In **20min** you have superb views of the Torres ahead and Pico da Nogueira, with its pipe, to the left. In **35min** Pico do Arieiro is just ahead; the Miradouro do Juncal is also prominent. Pass a clearing at the **Montado do Sabugal**, with two enormous fire-ravaged *til* trees. (On this walk you will see some of the oldest laurels on the island, with trunks over 8ft in diameter.) Two minutes past the clearing, a track joins from the left (❶; **40min**).

Walk a turns left down this track, in 10 minutes crossing a BRIDGE over the **Ribeira da Fajã da Nogueira**. Continue uphill for about 20 minutes, to a FORK NEAR THE KEEPERS' HOUSE (❷), where you ignore the track to the right. In **1h20min** you come to the top of the pipe, outside the UNDER-GROUND RESERVOIR (❸). Nearby is a grassy verge, perfect for picnicking. From here you overlook the sinuous Ribeira do Juncal and the Metade Valley. You're at 960m/3150ft; not far below, you can see an old levada that used to run between Balcões and Fajã da Nogueira, now completely crumbled away. Return the same way (**2h30min**); from the keepers' house, you could take a detour up left at ❷ (20min return), to see the levada and underground reservoir.

Walk b keeps ahead (right), climbing to the **Levada do Pico Ruivo** (❹; covered by a track; **1h10min**). Turn right, walking against the water's flow and coming to the setting shown below left. Past two keepers' houses and some short tunnels, at **1h40min** you enter a TUNNEL WITH RAILWAY TRACKS (❺; 12 minutes). You'll hear the roar of waterfalls on the far side before you exit by crashing falls and clear pools, high up in the **Ribeira Seca** (❻; **1h52min**). From this superb picnic spot the PICO RUIVO TUNNEL leads to Walk 23, but we turn back to the POWER STATION (❼; **3h40min**).

Left, Walk b: At 1h10min the Cabeço da Fajã dos Vinháticos is just in front of you; its velvety emerald ridges ripple down the north side of the Ribeira Seca. Right: The Alternative walk edges the Levada da Serra between the two tracks.

Walk 25: LEVADA DO FURADO FROM RIBEIRO FRIO TO LAMACEIROS AND PORTELA

See also photograph page 2   Distance: 11km/6.8mi; 3h25min

Grade: ● ‡‡ moderate, but you must be sure-footed and have a head for heights (***danger of vertigo***). Very popular route, recently upgraded, with sturdy railings — but railings often come down in storms. PR10

Equipment: walking boots or stout shoes that grip on slippery surfaces, long trousers, windproof, sunhat, fleece, plastic bottle/water purifying tablets, picnic, whistle

How to get there: 🚌 56, 103 or 138 to Ribeiro Frio
To return: 🚌 53 or 78 from Portela

Short walk: Ribeiro Frio — Balcões — Ribeiro Frio. ● 3km/2mi; 45-50min. Easy; 🚌 56, 103 or 138 or 🚗 to/from Ribeiro Frio (32° 44.107'N, 16° 53.178'W). The wide, signposted path (PR11) is below the souvenir shop. Follow it beside the dry levada, past a snack bar/souvenir stall. After passing through a cut in the towering basalt, you find yourself high in the Metade Valley. At a fork, where the old levada goes left (pictogram prohibiting walkers); turn right to the Balcões (**ⓐ**; *P25*) and superb views to the great peaks.

Alternative walks: grade, equipment, access as main walk

1 Ribeiro Frio — Ribeira do Poço do Bezerro — Chão das Feiteiras — Ribeiro Frio. ● ‡‡ 7.4km/4.6mi; 3h. Ascent (sometimes steep) of 300m/1000ft; equipment as main walk; *map inset opposite*. A five-star walk, ***but not suitable in heavy mist!*** 🚌 or 🚗 to/from Ribeiro Frio. Follow the main walk to **①** (1h), then clamber 2m/6ft up the bank and follow the path at the left of the right-hand levada channel straight uphill. This narrow old levada rises steeply to its source in the Ribeira do Poço do Bezerro (**ⓑ**; 2h; lovely pools). Retrace your steps for 30m/yds, then turn left up a narrow path (cairn). The path emerges from the trees on a sloping plateau (the Chão das Feiteiras). The odd, fairly large cairn marks the route as you follow a trodden path through ferns *(feiteiras)* — at first heading due west (over a crossing path) and then north-northwest — with a brilliant view to the high peaks. The path emerges by three farm buildings (**ⓒ**; 2h30min). Turn right in front of them but, after less than 200m, turn left on a grassy trail. Descend to the ER103, cross it, and pick up the continuing trail some 160m downhill. Beyond a picnic site and a cascading stepped levada, you emerge just above the trout farm (**ⓓ**; 3h).

2 Ribeiro Frio — Lamaceiros — Levada da Serra. ● ‡‡ Join the Levada da Serra at the Lamaceiros waterhouse: see Walk 10, page 70.

3 Ribeiro Frio — Pico do Suna — Portela. ● ‡‡ 13.5km/8.4mi; 4h 20min. Follow the main walk for 2h10min. Just after the tunnel, take the path on the left (**②**); fork left to climb above the tunnel, then keep straight up. Meeting a crossing trail, turn left up to the fire tower viewpoint at Pico do Suna (**ⓒ**; 30min). Retrace steps and continue to Portela.

This is a walk to which we return again and again, to enjoy the wonderful play of light and shade along the levada, the frisson of excitement at the Cabeço Furado, and the spectacular views in the second half of the walk.

Begin the walk just below the bar/restaurant at **Ribeiro Frio**. Here you will see a signpost, 'PR10, PORTELA' on your right (further downhill, on the left, is the sign for Balcões; *P25*). Here you join the fast-flowing **Levada do Furado** (**ⓞ**). In **20min** pass a tunnel on the right, where water is piped

It's a joy to follow the levada for just a short way, to revel in the play of light and shade over rocks and waterfalls, laurel and heath trees. The second part of the walk, beyond the Lamaceiros waterhouse, is completely different. You cross sunny pastures, enjoying pano-ramas of majestic moun-tains, proud valleys, and the tranquillity of the north coast villages in the distance.

into the levada. In **1h**, just by a bridge over the **Ribeira do Poço do Bezerro** (**1**), some fast-flowing watercourses join the main channel (*where Alternative walk 1 climbs the bank*). The finches here have been tamed by 'Landscapers' (see photo-graph on page 2), and will expect to be fed some titbits!

In **1h20min** you pass through four massive clefts in the rock, where concrete plates bridge the channel. Five minutes later pass a tiny SHRINE beside the levada. Soon there are splendid views left to the high peaks. At **2h** a path off left leads to a view over São Roque and Faial. At about **2h10min** you will pass through a very short tunnel. Just beyond it, a PATH (**2**) on the left doubles back over the levada and climbs to Pico do Suna (*Alternative walk 3*). Two minutes later you come to a precipice with railings, where the very narrow levada path is cut into the Suna escarpment at the **Cabeço Furado**. This excitement lasts for 10 minutes.

By **2h35min** you'll reach the **Lamaceiros** WATERHOUSE (**3**) and look out east to São Lourenço. (*From here Alternative walk 2 goes on to the Levada da Serra; there is also another path up to Pico do Suna.*) About 30m/yds past the waterhouse, turn left downhill beside the narrow **Levada da Portela** ... into a fairytale setting by a forestry house (picnic tables, tree ferns, toilets). A track takes you down past the emerald-green **Lagoa da Portela** below on the right. Fork left after 200m/yds (where a two-lane 'highway' descends to the reservoir!) and soon enjoy marvellous views of Faial, Penha de Águia and Porto da Cruz. When the levada goes right, stay on the track. After 250m, with a fenced-off property ahead (**4**), go left for 'PORTELA' at a signposted fork; the levada ist on your left. Soon slippery earthen steps take you down to the ER110. Walk left downhill to the **Portela** VIEWPOINT. Cross the road and descend steps to the ER212. The BUS STOP for Machico and Funchal is opposite the bar (**5**; **3h25min**).

Walk 26: CIRCUIT AROUND SANTANA

See map pages 98-99   **Distance:** 9km/5.6mi; 2h55min

Grade: ● moderate, with ascents/descents of about 200m/650ft overall. You must be sure-footed, but there is no danger of vertigo.

Equipment: stout shoes (walking boots preferable), sunhat, picnic, water

How to get there and return: 🚗 to Cortado, just east of Santana centre (32° 47.762'N, 16° 51.978'W) or 🚌 56, 103 or 138 to/from the 'Cortado–Santana' stop *(not all buses call there; check!)*

Short walks

1 **Pico da Boneca.** 3km/2mi; 50min. ● Easy. Access as main walk. Follow the main walk to the 50min-point, but continue back to Cortado.

2 **Levada do Cantinho.** 4.5km/2.8mi; 1h30min. ● Grade as main walk. Access: 🚌 *(bus times unsuitable)* to/from the chapel at Santo António, north of ❸ (32° 48.267'N, 16° 52.277'W). Descend the road opposite the chapel, picking up the main walk just past the 1h05min-point. Follow it back to ❸ (2h35min-point), then turn left for 320m, back to the chapel.

This gentle ramble round Santana takes you through lovely agricultural landscapes and opens up a wealth of coastal and inland views. And if you find the walk too 'tame', then interrupt it halfway along: take a 40 minute return detour to the cable car station, and enjoy the exhilarating ride down to Fajã da Rocha do Navio (Wed/Sat/Sun *only*)!

Start out at **Cortado** on the road to signposted to LAMA-CEIROS (**O**). After 120m/yds, turn off right on a track with a 'MIRADOURO' sign, below a house on the right. After 150m ignore a TUNNEL on the right (**❶**).* In **12min**, at a Y-fork, ignore the track up right to the antennas (you will return that way); keep ahead.** Some 300m/yds further on, climb a good zigzag path on the right to the trig point on **Pico da Boneca** (**❷; 25min**). Before you is the whole spread of Santana in the west and Faial in the east. But disappointingly, the high peaks behind Santana are *not* impressive from this perspective.

Leaving the peak, start down the path you ascended but, at a fork, keep left on a contouring path along the east side of the ridge, with fabulous views down over Faial and Eagle Rock, as well as the elongated wedge of Ponta do Clérigo. When the path comes to a pass below the antennas, turn right on a track. Follow this downhill to the junction encountered earlier, turn left and retrace your outgoing route.

Back at the tarred road (**50min**), follow it in a tight U-bend down to the right. Cross the **Ribeira de Santo António** and rise up to the road in **Santo António**, opposite a BUS SHELTER (**❸; 1h05min**). Note the cobbled trail at the left (initially

---

*You could go through this short tunnel and follow a narrow levada on the east side of the ridge (⁑); the path is very narrow and unstable in places.
**After 250m/yds you pass a path down left. It is an alternative to the route we use, but is very steep and overgrown (although we have been told that it is the *only* council-maintained path into the valley). If you take this, when you reach a levada, turn left, then take the path half-right almost immediately and pick up the main walk at just after the 1h05min-point.

View down over Fajã da Rocha do Navio from the Levada do Cantinho

tarred): it is your return route from Santana. Turn right and walk 300m/yds to a small CHAPEL on the right, then go left on the road opposite. As the road becomes concrete, go down steps and cross an access road to the expressway, then take a walkway past a thatched 'Santana house' on the right. Meeting a road, follow it down to a large, isolated house with a well-kept garden. Past the house, at the 'Stop' sign, turn right on the EXPRESSWAY ACCESS ROAD (④). Follow this straight over a roundabout until (after 200m) a sign indicates that drivers can make a U-turn. Here a gap in the roadside barrier to your left allows access to the **Levada do Cantinho** (**1h15min**).

Turn right on the clay path (slippery when wet) and follow the watercourse past cultivated plots and stands of sugar cane. You cross above the expressway and pass a concrete track off left, after which a brief diversion to the right leads to a goods hoist, from where you enjoy the splendid view shown above. (A short-cut path leads from here to the passenger cable car station; ⑤) Then the levada rounds the promontory below Covas, with a good view northwest to the Quinta do Furão and its vineyards. After again crossing above the expressway and another tunnel, watch for a sharp U-turn in the levada (where it seems to end in a thicket of cane).

Cross above the expressway again and almost at once meet a rough crossing concrete road in **Parlatorio** (⑥; **1h55min**). Turn left uphill here. (Or first detour 700m to the right, down to the cable car station.) At a fork, go straight ahead uphill (left, against the one-way traffic), making for a large 'silo'-shaped building. Curl up left past the front of the CHURCH in **Santana** (**2h05min**), then turn left on cobbles (RUA DR JOÃO DE ALMADA) and left again on asphalt (in front of a building with three flagpoles). Pass the SPORTS CENTRE on the right, ignore a road off left, and rise to a crossroads (⑦). Go straight over, at the left of the SCHOOL. The road descends, crosses a bridge, and immediately comes to crossroads. Go left here. The tar ends at once: ignore the steps to the left; take the grit track just to the right of them, going under a high arch. Drop down to cross the **Ribeira dos Pregos**, then rise up cobbled steps, back to BUS SHELTER in **Santo António** (③; **2h35min**). Now retrace your steps back up to **Cortado** (⓪; **2h55min**).

Walk 27: TWO WALKS FROM BOAVENTURA

Photograph page 29   Distance, etc: see Walks a and b below

Equipment: walking boots, sunhat, water, picnic, walking stick; extra fleece and windproof in cool weather, optional swimwear in summer

Walk a: Levada de Cima. ● ⁑ 5km/3mi; 1h45min. Moderate, with an ascent of only 40m/130ft and descent of 110m/350ft, but you must be sure-footed and have a head for heights; throughout, the levada path demands utmost concentration (***danger of vertigo***; there are *no* protective railings). Access: 🚌 6 or 🚗 to the viewpoint with shrine (32° 49.435'N, 16° 58.887'W) at Lombadinha above Ponta Delgada — a short way east of the red and white antenna (also with viewpoint). Return on 🚌 6 from Boaventura — back to base, or back to your car.

Walk b: Boaventura — Arco de São Jorge. ● ⁑ 4.1km/2.5mi; 1h 20min. Quite easy ascent of 180m/600ft; the Porco Valley will be very wet after heavy rain. *But very dangerous if the railings have come down and not yet been repaired.* Access: 🚌 6 to Boaventura; 🚌 103 to return (or bus 132 to Santana). 🚗: Motorists can do an out-and-back walk of 4km/ 2.5mi by parking at the Caminho do Calhau (32° 49.563'N, 16° 58.408'W) or the viewpoint with bar/restaurant at the end of the road (32° 49.609'N, 16° 58.379'W; see map); allow 2h and start at the 20min-point.

Two of the most delightful walks on the island! Walk a is a flower-filled hike past sunny promontories alternating with jungle-like stream crossings; it takes you along an ancient free-form levada. At the end of the walk, as you descend to Boaventura, you look out beyond the palm-shaded cemetery towards an old zigzag trail clinging precariously to a sugar-loaf cliff. It looks impossibly vertiginous, but *(provided that the railings are in place)* it's easy! Walk b takes you there.

Begin **Walk a** at the BUS STOP diagonally west downhill from the VIEWPOINT/SHRINE (◉). Climb the concrete steps a few paces east of the bus stop, to meet the **Levada de Cima** behind a lone house. First follow the levada to the *right:* in a minute you enjoy fine views west — as far as Ribeira da Janela. Five minutes later the levada drops over the cliff and into a tank; from here you overlook Ponta Delgada.

Now turn back, past the steps, and follow the levada south, remembering that this path will need your full concentration, so always *stop* to admire the views. When the levada disappears under concrete, keep ahead to cross a road at the hamlet of **Levada de Cima**, then take the second set of concrete steps (in front of a tiled tap) back down to the watercourse.

The first pocket of greenery is the most vertiginous, and even though the worst part is only 2m/yds across, Pat wades in the shallow levada; all the other vertiginous river crossings have diversionary paths. Like many old levadas, this one is not always corseted in concrete; it flows quickly and freely — sometimes shallow, sometimes deep ... through cultivation, under chestnuts, below dramatic cliffs.

At **Cabo da Ribeira (55min)** a concrete lane rises to the levada. Some five minutes later, stone-laid steps descend left.

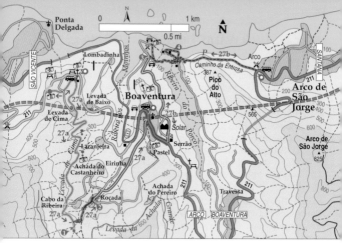

This is your return route, but first continue ahead to where the levada takes its source in the **Ribeira dos Moinhos**, a dark bowl brighted by cala lilies in spring (**①**; **1h05min**). Then return to the steps and descend across a BRIDGE to a wide path on the far side of the river. Follow this left, to a road in **Roçada**. Go left, then right, to walk just over 1km down to the CHURCH/BUS STOP in **Boaventura** (**○**; **1h45min**) — a beautiful stroll, looking out towards the valley and palm tree-fringed cemetery.

Walk b begins at the CHURCH (**○**) in **Boaventura**. Walk southeast along the ER211 towards Santana for 300m, then turn left in front of the electricity substation. Fork right almost at once, to pass the Solar (hotel) on your left. Some 1.2km down this road, descend the path on the right, the 'CAMINHO DO CALHAU' (**③**; **20min**).* After crossing the **Ribeira do Porco** on a stone bridge, it's worth exploring the picturesque old RUINS (**④**) to the left, above the mouth of the river — either take the narrow path on the left through a red clay gully (an awkward scramble at the outset) or bear right on the main path and, at a fork by a stone ruin, turn left. We *think* these are the remains of an old textile mill: our Madeiran history book refers to such ruins in this area, where 'fabric was made using the red clay obtained nearby'.

From the lone ruin the beautiful old trail (CAMINHO DA ENTROSA) rises in easy zigzags up the vertical cliff. The views straight down to the sea are breathtaking, but railings ensure no danger — unless they come down in storms (they *will* be repaired eventually; this is a popular walk with islanders proud of their heritage). Historians marvelled at the huge house leeks on these cliffs ('the size of hats'). The trail emerges at the Snack Bar Arco on the ER211 (**○**; **1h20min**; bus 103, 132).

*Motorists who park at the viewpoint/restaurant at the end of the road could access the walk from there: at the end of the road, take the rising path to the right that rounds a small plantation of sugar cane (*not* the trail on the left that descends to private property).

Map pages 98-99; photographs pages 39 (left) and 97

Distance: 8.8km/5.5mi; 2h45min

Grade: ● ∷ moderate-strenuous, with a descent of 550m/1800ft on a very steep and slippery path; you must be sure-footed; *not* recommended after heavy rain. Red and yellow waymarking (PR9, then PR1.1)

Equipment: walking boots, long trousers, sunhat, fleece, windproof, picnic, plastic bottle/water purifying tablets, walking stick

How to get there: 🚌 56, 103 or 138 to Santana, then 🚕 *taxi* to Queimadas
To return: 🚌 103 from Ilha de São Jorge

Alternative walk: ● ∷ Queimadas — Vale da Lapa — Queimadas. 10km/6.2mi; 3h05min. Quite easy, but grade as Walk 22 on the levada. Access/return: 🚗 car or *taxi* to/from Queimadas (or Pico das Pedras: see Short walk 21, page 95). Follow the main walk to the 1h25min-point, visit the tiny forestry house (**❷**), then return the same way.

Two walks in one: on this excursion you enjoy the shady meanderings of the Levada do Caldeirão Verde, and then you leave it for the sunny heights above São Jorge, with views of the north coast villages round to Santana.

Begin at **Queimadas** (**○**): follow WALK 22 for 1h, when you pass through a very short tunnel (you won't need a torch). Two minutes beyond the tunnel exit, take the path off right (**❶**; sign: 'ILHA, 3.8KM'). But after 20m/yds fork sharp left towards 'Pico Ruivo', *leaving* the Ilha path.* At the next junction, where the P1.1 goes left to Pico Ruivo, head right for 'Vale da Lapa', rising up a wide old ridge trail.

The views over the north coast from the small **Vale da Lapa** forestry house (*Posto florestal;* **❷**; **1h25min**) are fantastic — and the gardens are charming, with tree ferns amongst the other plants. To leave the forestry house pass to the left (west) of it on the old trail, which soon reverts to path. Be sure to bend right in a sharp U-turn after a couple of minutes (150m).

In five minutes the PR1.1 path joins from behind and to the right, then you descend log steps. The descent is steep and slippery, often beneath a bower of heath trees and ferns. On meeting a track (**1h40min**), follow it downhill. At a bend to the right, leave the track and walk ahead past a sign pointing back to Pico Ruivo. Descending a slippery (but romantic) SUNKEN PATH (**❸**), cross a track and follow the 'ILHA' sign. You join another track after 500m: descend for 70m, then go left where it bends sharply right (**❹**). Soon asphalt comes underfoot, and fingerposts point your way down to **Ilha** (**○**; **2h45min**). The BUS STOP is by the CHURCH and BAR.

*The Ilha path, the 'official' PR1.1 route, was once a beautiful stone-edged levada planted with hydrangeas. It offer fine views over the Levada do Caldeirão Verde and a lower levada in the same valley (Ribeira dos Arcos), but the channel has since been filled in with soil. Although there are railings at the exposed places, it is nevertheless vertiginous. We prefer to start this section via the Vale da Lapa forestry house.

111

Walk 29: LEVADA DA FAJÃ DO RODRIGUES

Photograph page 19   **Distance:** 6km/3.7mi; 2h25min

Grade: ● easy, level walking; some agility required; waymarked (PR16)

Equipment: stout lace-up shoes, sunhat, *torch*

How to get there and return: 🚌 to/from the levada: take the ER208 from Feiteiras (signs: 'Ginjas, Lanço, Parque Empresarial de São Vicente'; Car tours 1, 5). Keep following 'Parque Empresarial de São Vicente', going left at two T-junctions (0.9km, 2.4km). At 3.5km you pass this unused industrial estate, on the left. Park nearby or continue up rough track for another 400m, to park by the signpost for PR16 (32° 46.753'N, 17° 2.970'W).

The Fajã do Rodrigues Levada used to be too dangerous to follow very far upstream, but since its upgrading everyone can now explore some of this beautiful wilderness, abounding with ancient laurels, ferns and birdsong.

Start out at the PR16 SIGNPOST (**○**) beside the **Levada da Fajã do Rodrigues** and follow the levada to the right. You come to a huge SLUICE, where water from a 1.5km-long tunnel bored into the rock on the left pours into the levada (**4min**) — a tremendously invigorating spot!

Threading your way below eucalyptus and beside a plethora of vegetation, you penetrate a deep valley, where the laurel-coated pinnacles of the **Furna da Areia** tower above you. A good pumice path has come under foot, flanked by steel railings. Twenty minutes from the sluice you reach a *caldeirão* (**❶; 24min**), a high rock basin where a narrow waterfall drops almost 200m/650ft (if it hasn't been such a dry year that it's dried up!). You won't get *too* wet splashing below it, and it's worth continuing along the levada *through* the first short TUNNEL (**❷; 35min;** *torch required*). (The levada takes its source 2km northwest in the Ribeira do Inferno; much of it flows through tunnels, the last one 1100m long.)

Return the same way, catching glimpses down left of the lovely view shown on page 19. From the SLUICE (**1h**) continue southeast along the levada, past lily-of-the-valley trees, purple glory bushes and a few cottages with vegetable plots and tiny apple orchards. You pass two sunny promontories with beautiful views over the terraced valley north of Rosário before reaching a TUNNEL in the **Ribeira da Vargem** (**❸; 1h45min;** *see map on the reverse of the touring map*), from where this levada flows over 3km to the power station at Serra de Água. Now return the same way to the PR16 SIGNPOST (**○; 2h25min**).

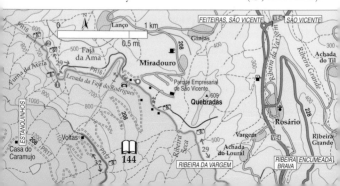

144

Walk 30: LOMBADA DA PONTA DO SOL • LEVADA NOVA • RIBEIRA DA TÁBUA • RIBEIRA BRAVA

Map pages 114-115; photograph page 34

Distance: 13km/8mi; 3h50min

Grade: ● ‼ moderate-strenuous, with an overall ascent of 200m/650ft and a steep descent of 400m/1300ft at the end of the walk. You must be sure-footed and have a head for heights (*danger of vertigo* on the levada).

Equipment: stout shoes or walking boots, long trousers, sunhat, picnic, water, walking stick; extra fleece and windproof in cool weather

How to get there: 🚌 142 to Formiga (Fohr-**mee**-gah; it means 'ant'!) on the ER222, 2.1km east of the turn-off to Ponta do Sol

To return: 🚌 any suitable bus from Ribeira Brava

Alternative walk: Lombada's levadas. ● ‼ Distance optional; *expert;* equipment as main walk (*plus torch*). Access: 🚌 as above or 🚗 to/from Lombada (32° 41.351'N, 17° 5.514'W). Two levadas take their source high on the eastern flanks of the Ribeira da Ponta do Sol; *both are vertiginous, the old one extremely so, although both have been recently repaired.* Explore the old Levada do Moinho from the church (❶), then return and follow the main walk to the Levada Nova (❷). Pursue this newer levada up the valley as far as you can. *Experts* make a circuit — up the valley on one levada and back along the other; steps connect the two near their sources.

The rose-pink *solar* at Lombada was for centuries the largest country house on Madeira. And it stood in the largest private estate — the Lombada dos Esmeraldos, stretching from the Paúl da Serra down to the sea between the Ponta do Sol and Caixa valleys. This huge domain had been given by Zarco to one of his sons, who cultivated sugar cane with great success. It was later bought by João de Esmeraldo, a friend of Christopher Columbus. At one time 80 slaves worked in Esmeraldo's plantations and mills; with the wealth created, he built the mansion and nearby church of the Espírito Santo. There is little evidence of the sugar plantations today, but the valleys are still a tapestry of cultivation.

Start out at **Formiga** (⊙): climb the road to **Lombada** (❶; see map; **20min**). Look at the old *solar*, then enjoy the superb view over the **Ribeira da Ponta do Sol** (photograph page 34) from the balcony walkway behind the CHURCH. Here an iron gate leads to the old (1400s) **Levada do Moinho**; it powered the mills in the sugar plantations. To reach the new levada, start back out of Lombada the way you came in, heading east on the road between the church and the *solar*, then take the second left turn (a narrow asphalt road). Follow this quite steeply uphill to a T-junction*, where you turn left for 50m/yds, then right alongside the **Levada Nova** (❷; **35min**; sign).

Now begin to pace out Esmeraldo's domain. Five minutes along, weave between the houses of **Jangão**, then descend steps to a narrow road, with a building opposite. Go straight over this road, following another road (CAMINHO DO JANGÃO) just to the right of the building (a shop). After 150m/yds

*The Alternative walk heads *left* 70m/yds *before* the T-junction.

(after the fourth lamp post, by house 124), descend steps back to the levada. In winter and spring calla lilies and yellow-blooming vetch are a perfect foil for the dark rods of sugar cane still cultivated here (probably for the spirit, *aguardente*).

After crossing a concrete path you come into the **Ribeira da Caixa**, soon passing through a very short TUNNEL. The cane peters out as you leave Esmeraldo's ridge, to be replaced by willow, the odd banana grove, and all the ingredients for a hearty vegetable soup. Ten minutes past the tunnel you come to a waterfall chasm at the head of the valley. If the sturdy BRIDGE (❸) here has been destroyed, use the detour path down in the valley (violet line on our map).

Ten minutes later (**1h15min**) you leave the valley, coming to a road. Cross over and continue on the levada. Only a minute later a CONCRETE TRACK (❹) crosses the levada; follow this track 20m/yds downhill to the right, then rejoin the channel (with street lights) on the left. Now head north into the **Ribeira da Tábua**, graced with white iris, broom and sugar cane in spring, hayricks, sweet chestnuts and black-berries in autumn. The levada is quite sluggish here. Beyond a sugar cane grove, in **Ribeira da Tábua** village, you cross a bridge and then ford a SPILLWAY* (❺; **2h05min**). Heading southeast, cross the village road on steps; a SNACK BAR is up to the left. After passing through a cut in the basalt cliffs (**2h15min**), where stepping stones bridge the levada, you enjoy the best views of this valley — its river pools, poplars and hay-ricks. But along here the path is very vertiginous.

A short TUNNEL (❻; **2h20min**) takes you into a new valley, and after crossing a road, you pass a grassy knoll on the right overlooking coastal Tábua. In under **2h45min** the levada disappears beneath a walkway. Turn left up concrete steps, to **Corujeira** (there is a BAR here), where a road descends to the ER222. Follow the road downhill to the right for 100m/yds, to where the levada continues on a high parapet. This is so vertiginous that it is easier to walk down the road: keep left at the junction quickly encountered. Just past the junction, the road makes a U-bend in the **Ribeira da Caldeira**. Here take the *second* set of STEPS on your right (❼), to descend to the levada. You meet a narrow CONCRETE ROAD (❽; **3h**): turn right and follow WALK 31 from just after its 4h35min-point, dropping steeply to **Ribeira Brava** (❾; **3h-50min**).

*If the spillway is too wet, take the concrete steps just before it and turn right on the road, back down to the levada.

Walk 31: ENCUMEADA • LEVADA DO LOMBO DO MOURO • RIBEIRA BRAVA

Map begins on the reverse of the touring map and ends below

Distance: 15.5km/9.6mi; 5h25min

Grade: ● ‼ strenuous, with a climb of 300m/985ft to start (but see 'How to get there' below) and a very steep descent of 1300m/4265ft. You must be sure-footed; much of the route can be *very* overgrown.

Equipment: walking boots, long sleeves/trousers, sunhat, fleece, windproof, picnic, plastic bottle/water purifying tablets, whistle, walking stick

How to get there: 🚌 6 or 139 to Encumeada Pass (*not* the Residencial Encumeada), or 🚕 *taxi* from Ribeira Brava or São Vicente to the Lombo do Mouro house access road on the ER105, 4.1km up from Encumeada Pass (32° 44.220N, 17° 2.975'W), in which case deduct 4.1km/1h30min.

To return: 🚌 any suitable bus from Ribeira Brava

The Lombo do Mouro, a dinosaur's back of a ridge, is the setting for a delightful levada walk … but save it until you've acquired your 'Madeira knees'—the descent to Ribeira Brava will leave them quaking!

Start out at **Encumeada** (○): walk to the north side of the pass and climb the ER105 to the **Lombo do Mouro** access road, on your left after just over 4km (❶; **1h30min**). Follow the road to its end, then keep down the grassy path and precarious steps. Just before this beautifully sited government

Ribeira Brava (left); the rushing levada and the Lombo do Mouro house, below the escarpment of the Paúl da Serra (Picnic 31)

rest house and hunting lodge, you join the **Levada do Lombo do Mouro** (❷; **1h40min**; *P*31). Follow its flow, initially via a 'cauldron'-like valley prone to landslides (❸), where the levada is briefly encased in plastic piping and you may have to cross a couple of rockfalls. There are fine views east towards Pico Grande (Walk 4), Chão dos Terreiros (Walk 5) and the Arieiro/ Ruivo route (Walk 19). Go through a gate in **2h10min** and then perhaps take a break in the tall golden grass, with orange butterflies pursuing the purple thistles and foxgloves, and the levada surging down beside you. Put on protective clothing: the next stretch is often *very* overgrown.

In **2h40min** you come into the EUCALYPTUS ZONE (❹), so you know that you have already dropped to below 900m/ 3000ft. Five minutes later the levada describes a WIDE ARC (❺) and descends very steeply (photograph above).

From time to time you will be aware of a track sidling up to the levada and eventually you're forced to join it. It takes you to a road, by a large WATER TANK on the right (❻; **3h55min**). Turn left for a little over 200m/yds, then go right, down a steep concrete track. When you join another road, follow it downhill for 375m/yds, then go left on concrete (❼). From here on, always take the steepest route downhill, with the dramatic **Brava Valley** close by on your left.

At **4h35min** cross straight over another asphalt road; 60m/yds further down, WALK 30 comes in from the right (❽), in front of a garage. Beyond a stretch of concrete steps which cross yet another road, turn left at a junction (**4h45min**). At another junction, keep left down more concrete steps (❾; **4h55min**). Meeting the ER222, go left downhill and find the final flight of steps down into **Ribeira Brava** (◯; **5h25min**). Cross the bridge over the river; the CHURCH is opposite; the 'BUS STATION' runs north along the road in front of it.

Walk 32: FOLHADAL AND THE NORTE AND RABAÇAS LEVADAS

Map on reverse of touring map **Distance:** 10.2km/6.2mi; 2h50min

Grade: ● ∷ easy, but you must be sure-footed and have a head for heights (*danger of vertigo* on the Levada das Rabaças). Two tunnels (one fairly long). The levada walk to Folhadal is part of the PR17.

Equipment: stout shoes, good torch *for each member of the party*, sunhat, plastic bottle/water purifying tablets, picnic, fleece, windproof

How to get there and return: 🚌 6 or 139 to Encumeada *pass* (*not* the Residencial Encumeada); 🚌 6 to return. Or 🚗: park at the viewpoint on the north side of the pass (32° 45.271N, 17° 1.205'W; Car tours 1 and 5).

Short walk: Encumeada — Folhadal — Encumeada. ● ∷ 4km/2.5mi; 1h. Equipment, access/return as above. Follow the main walk to Folhadal (**②**) and back. *A 5-star walk on a fine day; the paths are amply wide, and there is little danger of vertigo, but good torches are essential.*

Alternative walks

1   Encumeada — ER208 — Encumeada. ● ∷ 18.6km/11.5mi; 4h 50min. Follow the main walk to the second tunnel (**③**; 45min) and go through. When the PR17 goes off right, keep ahead through two more tunnels, to a pretty waterhouse on the ER208 (**④**); allow 2h return (50min in tunnels); see purple arrows on the map. There are protective railings at most exposed points. Then finish the main walk.

2   Encumeada — Cascalho — Encumeada. ● ∷ 19.5km/12mi; 4h. *Expert:* very narrow levada paths, some unprotected (*danger of vertigo*); at least two potentially hazardous screes; one *very long, often very wet tunnel*. Access/return/equipment as above (but wear walking boots and long trousers and take a whistle). Follow the main walk for 2h, then go through the long tunnel (**⑤**; 2.3km; *at least* 30min), to emerge in the Ponta do Sol Valley. Cascalho (**⑥**; 3h; 'Scree') is one of the sources of the Rabaças levada. Further on, the levada has collapsed (see page 126; Cascalho itself can no longer be reached from Walk 35b). Return direct to Encumeada.

P ower and majesty. These may be your first impressions when you step onto the levada at Encumeada Pass. You are at the centre of the deep north/south cleft that splits the island. The high peaks rise in the east; the magnificent valley

Left (top and bottom): Levada do Norte path to Folhadal. Right: looking east towards Pico Grande from the Levada das Rabaças. Fog is pouring out of the tunnel where the Levada do Norte comes in from Folhadal.

of Serra de Água lies to the south. And at your feet, the Levada do Norte, 1.5m/5ft deep and just as wide, surges along in a massive concrete channel. You're bound for Folhadal, a primeval wonderland of ferns and ancient laurels.

Start the walk opposite the bar/restaurant, on the south side of the pass at **Encumeada** (**○**), where a blue and yellow sign indicates 'FOLHADAL'. Climb concrete steps here up to the **Levada do Norte (with an information board for the PR17)** and follow it westwards, past the keepers' flower-filled house. You'll be amazed by the abundance of vegetation: conifers of every description, heath and hawthorn, with a tangle of laurel, azaleas, lilies, hydrangeas, and myriad wild flowers. If you're walking here in June, you'll see the splendid cornflower-blue 'Pride of Madeira' in all its glory. In **12min** you come to the promontory of **Lapa do Galho** (*P*32): from here you enjoy fine views down over the valley and the south coast. You can also see the levada continuing to the east and emptying into the metal pipe down to the power station (inaugurated in 1953). There are 50km/31mi of channels north of here (including 11km/6.8mi of tunnels). From the power station the water flows on in another 35km/22mi of channels (7km/4.5mi of tunnels) to irrigate the terraces of Ribeira Brava and Câmara de Lobos (see Walk 6).

Past the promontory the levada forks. Turn right here and follow the Levada do Norte into the TUNNEL (**❶**; **14min**), which will take about 10-12 minutes to pass through. We'll never forget our first walk here: we approached the tunnel to find what looked like a washing machine gone mad. Thick white 'foam' was pouring out of it (see photograph on the previous page) — fog, rushing through from the other side!

The TUNNEL EXIT (**❷**; **25min**) frames your first glimpse of **Folhadal**, a 'museum' of ferns and indigenous trees — *vinháticos, til* trees (laurels) and white-barked *paus brancos* (olive family). But your eyes will be drawn to the *folhados* for which this wood is named — the summer-flowering lily-of-the-valley trees, native only to Madeira. Keep ahead through the *laurisilva*, enjoying views to the São Vicente valley — until you come to a second tunnel (**45min**). From here return* the same way to the levada fork (**1h15min**).

Now turn right to follow the narrower **Levada das Rabaças** (1970), a 'tributary' of the Levada do Norte. It is flowing in from Cascalho, the waterfall basin explored in Walk 35b (and the Alternative walk). In **1h45min** a waterfall on the right heralds a short TUNNEL (**❹**; 3min to pass). Seven minutes later, you reach a lonely keepers' house above the Pousada dos Vinháticos. When you come to the LONG TUNNEL (**❺**; **2h**) to Cascalho (*Alternative walk*), turn back to the 'FOLHADAL' SIGN/BUS STOP at **Encumeada** (**○**; **2h50min**).

Walk 33: BICA DA CANA • LEVADA DA SERRA • PINÁCULO • BICA DA CANA

Map on reverse of touring map; see also photograph page 19

Distance: 6.5km/4mi; 2h05min

Grade: ● ░░, with a descent/re-ascent of about 150m/500ft. You must be sure-footed and have a head for heights (*danger of vertigo*), although the exposed points were well protected at time of writing. *The walk is potentially very dangerous if the fencing has come down.* Mostly PR17

Equipment: walking boots, long trousers, sunhat, fleece, windproof, picnic, plastic bottle/water purifying tablets, whistle

How to get there and return: ⛟ to/from Bica da Cana (32° 45.451'N, 17° 3.565'W; Car tour 5)

Alternative walk: ER105 — Pináculo — Bica da Cana. 5km/3mi; 1h45min. ● ░░ Moderate-strenuous ascent of 400m/1300ft; the path (PR17) is well protected at time of writing, but all the comments about grade above apply. ⛟ Ask friends to drop you on the ER105, 3.3km uphill from Encumeada, where the road crosses the Levada do Lombo do Mouro (ⓐ; *not* signed at press date). Arrange to be collected later by the PR17 walkers' signboard at the entrance drive to the Bica da Cana refuge (ⓞ). From the ER105 climb steps and follow the Levada do Lombo do Mouro to the right. Beyond its source, a zigzag path takes you up to the Levada da Serra (ⓑ). Turn right; you will reach Pináculo (ⓢ) in 1h. Continue on the levada, *past* a path up left to Bica da Cana (ⓒ; perhaps with a cairn), and then the levada's source (ⓔ). Under 35min from Pináculo, turn left uphill on a path with a PR17 sign for Bica da Cana (ⓘ). Here you *leave* the PR17, which continues ahead to Caramujo.

O ne of our all-time favourite walks, absolutely gorgeous in its own right … and affording a splendid outlook towards the high peaks. You're just on the eastern flanks of the Paúl da Serra, and you'll enjoy the laughter of a vigorous levada and the falls that feed it.

Start out on the ER105, by the WALKERS' SIGNBOARD for the PR17 (ⓞ) at left of the entrance drive to the **Bica da Cana** refuge. Descend the clear earthen path, continuing straight down over a faint crossing path (which you may not even notice). Where the trail bends hard left, *ignore* a path off right (it's a cul-de-sac). But *do* turn right a minute or so later — at

Below Bica da Cana, Pináculo (on the right, in the middle distance) rises above heath trees. Fog engulfs São Vicente's valley, but the peaks in the east (Walk 19) are bathed in sun.

a T-junction with a wide, level path (PR17 signpost pointing back the way you came, left to Caramujo/Encumeada and right to Lombo do Mouro). Now you're on the sometimes overgrown and very wet (even in high summer!) PR17 path to Pináculo (**❶; 12min**).

In **30min** you reach the SOURCE of the **Levada da Serra** (**❷**), where wild carrots and *Senecio* spill down the cliff. Four-five minutes further on you pass some railings and steps up to the right into a tiny *caldeirão*. About 100m further on, *watch for* your ongoing path back to Bica on the right (**❸**; there *may* be a cairn). But for now continue on the levada, past golden grasses ablaze with foxgloves and butterflies. Below in the São Vicente valley is the chapel of Nossa Senhora de Fátima (photograph page 19). Hawks circle watchfully above.

Almost at once you come to the most spectacular part of the trail, where you walk below WATERFALLS (**❹**) foaming down a high basalt rock face. This short stretch, currently well protected, would be *very dangerous* if the railings are down. (Half the cliff has come down since we first walked here!) Beyond an even larger waterfall is the giant basalt **Pináculo** (**❺; 45min**). Continue along the levada as long as you like — perhaps for another 15 minutes — just to enjoy the negative ions, the flowers, and the views.

Before you lose height, turn back. Pass 'the Pinnacle' (**1h20min**) and, on reaching the path spotted earlier (10m past a clearing, when approached from this direction), turn left up the good, initially steep and sometimes stepped path (**1h30min**). Rise up to a fork on a wide SADDLE (**❻; 1h40min**) and turn right uphill. Head up towards the Bica da Cana view-point, where two isolated trees stand out as landmarks (even in fog) and continue up the clear path below the trees. Visit the **Bica da Cana** VIEWPOINT (**P33**), then follow the skiddy pumice track back to the cobbled Bica entrance drive and then your car at the PILLARS (**❼; 2h05min**).

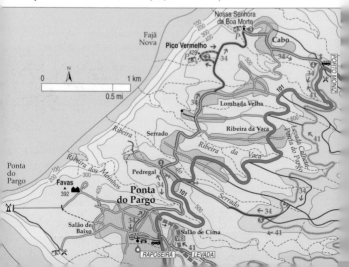

Walk 34: CIRCUIT AROUND PONTA DO PARGO

Map opposite; photos page 135   Distance: 13.2km/8.2mi; 4h

Grade: ● easy, with ascents/descents of 250m/820ft overall. Note that the levada may be dry outside summer months.

Equipment: stout shoes, sunhat, windproof, fleece, picnic, water

How to get there and return: 🚌 80, 142, 150 or 🚗 to/from Ponta do Pargo (32° 48.685'N, 17° 14.845'W; Car tour 6), or 🚗 to/from Nossa Senhora da Boa Morte (32° 49.928'N, 17° 14.086'W). Or, to avoid the climb from Cabo, do the walk in reverse from the levada crossing north of Lombada dos Marinheiros (see touring map; 🚌 or 🚗 to 32° 47.265'N, 17° 14.031'W).

This lovely ramble follows a country road from Ponta do Pargo to Cabo and takes in a short stretch of the Levada Calheta–Ponta do Pargo (see also Walk 41). The only disadvantage is the 25-minute climb to the levada. A good option is to start further south (see above) and avoid the climb! *Note:* the golf course planned for this area has been abandoned.

Start the walk at the CHURCH in **Ponta do Pargo** (**O**). With the church on your left, walk left down the road signposted to Salão de Baixo, but turn right immediately on RUA CARREIRA DE CIMA — before the large civic centre with the CENTRO DE SAUDE. When you come to a crossroads (to the lighthouse), walk a few paces to the right uphill but, just before reaching the ER101, go left downhill, passing a garage on the left with a tiled door frame. The road descends, crosses the **Ribeira dos Moinhos**, and rises into **Pedregal**, where you pass a TAP on the right ('CMC'; **①; 30min**).

Continue along the gently undulating road through **Serrado** (notice the beautifully carved façade of a derelict house on the right) and then **Lombada Velha**, where a Canary palm graces the first house and a beautiful old manor stands off to the left, shaded by a huge eucalyptus. Beyond this hamlet keep left along an earthen track. It's worth forking left to the trig point at **Pico Vermelho** (**②**), for the view back towards the lighthouse and Pico das Favas (with the antenna).

The track rises to the chapel of **Nossa Senhora da Boa Morte** (**③; 1h35min**). The modern building is unremarkable, but its grassy setting is idyllic — as the contented cows will agree! There is a *miradouro* nearby. From the chapel follow the asphalt road uphill through **Cabo** to the ER101. Just *before* the main road, by a large WATER TANK on your left, turn right on the **Levada Calheta–Ponta do Pargo** (**④; 2h**). The levada crosses the main road in seven minutes, then runs inland. Follow its meanderings for under an hour. Past a large WATER TANK and four minutes after crossing the **Ribeira do Serrado** on a narrow levada 'bridge', turn right down a track/then road (**⑤; 3h**). Descend to the ER101 (by a tap on the right), cross the road and continue straight down, back to the old road in **Pedregal** (**①**). Turn left, past the TAP encountered earlier. Retrace your steps to **Ponta do Pargo** (**O; 4h**).

Walk 35: LEVADA DO PAÚL AND LEVADA DA BICA DA CANA

Distance, grade, equipment, access: see individual walks below

Walk a: Levada do Paúl west from Campo Grande, then down to Loreto. 16.6km/10.3mi; 4h55min. ● : easy-moderate, narrow levada path *(possibility of vertigo)*. Wear stout shoes (walking boots preferable), sunhat, windproof, fleece; carry picnic, plastic bottle/water purifying tablets, *strong torch*. Access by 🚌 115 or 142 to Recta das Canhas ('**Ray**-tah dahs **Kahn**-yahs'), where there is a taxi rank. Ask the driver to take you to Cristo Rei, Campo Grande (**Kreesh**-toh **Ray**, **Kam**-poh **Grahnd**). Return on 🚌 80, 115 or 142 from Loreto.

Shorter versions of Walk a

1 **Levada do Paúl.** Follow the levada west as far as you like — perhaps to the caves and back. 5km/3mi; 1h30min. ● : Grade and equipment as above (but no torch). Best access is by 🚗 (a detour on Car tour 5; park at the forestry house above Cristo Rei (32°44.393'N, 17°6.038'W) and follow the ER209 south for 300m/yds to the levada. *The path may be very wet!*

2 **Rabaçal — Loreto.** ● : 9.8km/6mi; 3h40min. Grade, equipment, access as main walk. Ask the taxi driver to take you to the Rabaçal turn-off on the ER105; join the main walk at ❸, just after the 1h15min-point.

Walk b: Levada da Bica da Cana and Levadas das Rabaças east from Campo Grande. 8.8km/5.5mi; 3h. ● :: moderate, with a descent and re-ascent of 320m/1050ft; you must be sure-footed and have a head for heights (*danger of vertigo*). Equipment as Walk a, plus walking stick(s). Access as Shorter version 1 of Walk a.

Alternative version of Walk b: Levada da Bica da Cana. 11km/6.8mi; 3h. ● :: Fairly easy climb/descent of 130m/425ft, but *danger of vertigo* on the narrow levada path. Equipment, access as main Walk b. Follow the walk for 40min, to ❻, then continue on the levada, to climb to its source just below the Paúl da Serra (❶; 1h35min). Return the same way.

Although the fires in Funchal made the news in August 2016, a huge swathe of the Paúl da Serra south of the ER105 was also devastated. Walks a and b used to be two separate walks, but we would not recommend either for the duration of this edition. However, we have included the bare bones of the routes because these walks are so popular. Perhaps in a few years' time the situation will be less bleak.

Walk a: The taxi will deposit you on **Campo Grande**, 9km up the road from Canhas, just below a statue of Christ the King ('CRISTO REI'). Here the ER209 crosses the **Levada do Paúl** (❶), one of the island's older levadas, now integrated into the new scheme. Further east it is more accurately called the Levada da Bica da Cana (Walk b), for it takes its source below Bica da Cana, in the Ribeira da Ponta do Sol. **Begin** by walking west beside a perhaps empty levada. The hideous SOLAR FARM at the outset pales into insignificance when contrasted with the desolation of the charred landscape (as we go to press). At **55min** caves stretch up into the hills on the right — shelter for animals and shepherds back in the days when cows grazed these slopes.

After crossing a road, at about **1h10min** you'll see the large hotel at Urze up to the right, and a metal pipe in the distance. The pipe is carrying water from the reservoir above Rabaçal down to the Calheta power station. The turbines of this station (commissioned 1953) feed on water from five separate levadas: you are walking one of them now, Walk 38

*The Alternative version of Walk b climbs 130m/425ft to the source of the levada, sometimes on steps. Experienced walkers, **equipped with a compass**, could scramble from the source up the stream bed and make their way to Bica da Cana, to be met by friends (see map on reverse of the touring map). But for the average walker, who has left a car at Cristo Rei, this would be **exceedingly dangerous**: fog comes down like a curtain! Remember, the levada is your **only** guide back to your car, and it is unlikely that you would be able to find it again, unless you are an expert with compass or GPS. Below: the blue ribbon of the Levada do Paúl as it was before the fires.*

introduces a second, and Walk 37 explores the other three. From the power station the water is sent eastwards to irrigate the fields of Calheta (14km/8.7mi of channels) and westwards to Ponta do Pargo (40km/25mi of channels). Walks 34 and 41 amble along this levada.

Eventually you come to a tiny CHAPEL (**1h15min**). The levada continues into the reservoir, from where it is piped down to the power station. Cross the ER105, where you will see the **Levada do Alecrím** (Walk 38) below the road. Walk left, to a LARGE PARKING AREA (🅐), then take the narrow road (PR6 and PR6.1; closed to traffic) down towards Rabaçal. Now north of the ER105, you're surrounded by greenery! After crossing the **Ribeira do Alecrím** with its lovely pools (**1h25min**), continue downhill under the watchful eyes of goats until you arrive at **Rabaçal**, a government rest house (**1h40min**; 🅞 — starting point for Walk 37).

When the tarred road ends, turn right down a paved track to the **Levada do Risco**. Follow the track beside it for five minutes, then fork left down a path, to the **Levada das 25 Fontes**. Turn left when you reach this levada, following the flow (both of these levadas are explored at leisure in Walk 37). Fifteen minutes' walking along this enchanting watercourse will bring you to a grassy sun-trap outside the entrance to the first major TUNNEL (🅑) built on Madeira, in the mid 1800s (notice the poignant shrine). It takes under 20 minutes to pass through this very high tunnel, built to accommodate people on horseback. Unfortunately, today we have to share the path with an intrusive shoulder-high water pipe.

Soon you've left the greenery of Rabaçal for the fire-blackened heights of Calheta's *lombos,* where you'll find a KEEPERS' COTTAGE (🅒: probably burnt out, we didn't have time to check), a rustic picnic table and a TAP. *Before* you reach the cottage, continue left along the levada for about 50m/yds, until it flows under a rock overhang. Here descend and cross a narrow concrete bridge. Then head downhill to the right on a path. In **2h50min** you will meet two pipes carrying water from the tank down

123

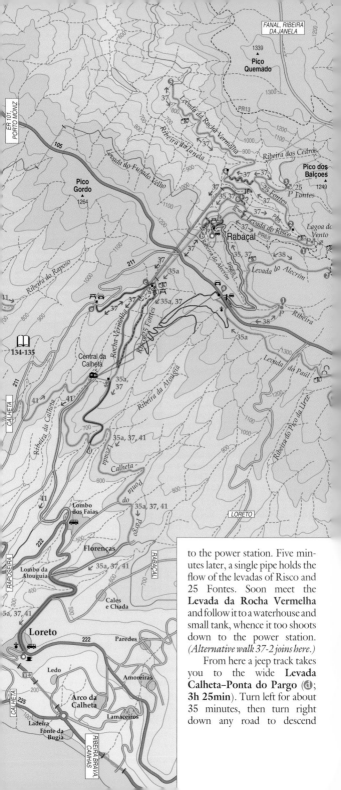

Pico
Quemado
1339

Pico dos
Balçoes
1249

Pico
Gordo
1264

Levada da Rocha Vermelha

Ribeira da Janela

Ribeira dos Cedros

Levada do Furado Velho

ER 101,
PORTO MONIZ

105

P Fontes

Fontes

Rabaçal

Levada do Risco

Lagoa do
Vento

Ribeira do Alecrim

Levada do Alecrim

211

Ribeira do Raposo

Rocha Vermelha

Risco/25 Fontes

134-135

Central da
Calheta

Ribeira da Atougia

Levada da Paul

Levada
Calheta -
Ponta
do
Passo

35a, 37, 41

LORETO

CALHETA

211

Lombo
dos Faias

Florenças

RAPOSEIRA

Lombo da
Atouguia

RABAÇAL

Cales
e Chada

Loreto

222

Paredes

Ledo

Amoreiras

VE3

Arco da
Calheta

CALHETA

225

Lamaceiros

Ladeira
Fonte da
Bugia

RIBEIRA
BRAVA
CANHAS

to the power station. Five minutes later, a single pipe holds the
flow of the levadas of Risco and
25 Fontes. Soon meet the
Levada da Rocha Vermelha
and follow it to a waterhouse and
small tank, whence it too shoots
down to the power station.
(Alternative walk 37-2 joins here.)

From here a jeep track takes
you to the wide **Levada
Calheta–Ponta do Pargo** (d;
3h 25min). Turn left for about
35 minutes, then turn right
down any road to descend

through **Florenças**. When you meet the main ER222 (**4h25min**), turn left and follow it to **Loreto**'s plane-shaded centre (⊙) and chapel, reached in about **4h55min**. The BUS stops here.

Walk b: Our goal on this route used to be Cascalho — a primeval wonderland, a hidden bowl of waterfalls where the Ribeira da Ponta do Sol gathers its strength and now feeds the Levada das Rabaças. Cascalho is still accessible from the east, from Encumeada, via a 2.3km-long tunnel (Alternative walk 32), but *not* from this *westerly* route. So our goal on this walk is now a *caldeirão* just short of Cascalho — but no less impressive!
We begin on the ER209, 300m/yds below the statue of 'CRISTO REI' (⊙): head east on the **Levada da Bica da Cana**, which may well still be empty (Walk a heads west here). In **23min** you cross an old cobbled trail (it descends to the ER222 in 9km/6mi). On the far side of the trail the levada path starts to climb. The climb levels out two minutes later, passing a viewpoint down the **Ribeira da Ponta do Sol**. Below, to the right,

you'll spot your track down to the *caldeirão*. Go through a gate and continue on the narrow path.

At **40min** you come to the CROSSING TRACK (**f**) seen from above: turn down right. The descent is quite gradual, but the rubble underfoot is treacherous. Soon you are descending beside the **Levada das Rabaças**. From a promontory with WORKMEN'S SHED (**1h**) there's a view down over Lombada on a hilltop in the valley, with its rosy *solar* and white chapel (Walk 30). Continue through the short S-shaped TUNNEL (**g**) at the left of the shed, and *use your torch:* the levada *crosses* the track in the tunnel.

Out of the tunnel, you soon reach a huge basin. You could be forgiven for thinking yourself at Cascalho, so impressive is this wilderness. Continue downhill with the levada, past several sluices and water pits, then past a TUNNEL (**1h15min**). Some cable fencing allays feelings of vertigo now. Finally, at **1h20min**, you reach FOUR LARGE WATER PIPES (**h**) which are carried across the cauldron by cables — replacing the levada channel that was ripped from the rock face in the 2010 storms. Allow an additional five minutes, if you walk on to the end of the old levada channel.

Then return the same way to the ER209 (**◉**; **3h**).

Walk 36: for almost the entire walk you will be overlooking the Seixal Valley on the north coast (as below) or the valley of the Ribeira da Janela to the south. The Fanal is our favourite place on the island — not only on account of the exquisite centuries-old til trees like the one shown on page 8, but for the myriad lime-green trails. They sparkle in the sun and are little eroded — probably because relatively few people are using them. You may find it hard to believe, but when we first walked from Boca da Corrida to Boca do Cerro (Walk 4), the trail was very like those in the Fanal — wide, flat, grassy and mossy…

Walk 36: FANAL CIRCUIT

See photograph opposite

Distance: 4.6km/2.8mi; 1h25min

Grade: ● very easy, with ups and downs of about 100m/330ft overall. *But not recommended in fog or for people who are frightned by cows.* PR13

Equipment: stout shoes (boots preferably; the paths can be muddy), fleece, long trousers, sunhat, windproof, picnic, water

How to get there and return: 🚌 to/from the Fanal forestry house, off the ER209 (Car tour 5; 32° 48.544'N, 17° 8.489'W)

The Fanal is probably our very favourite place on Madeira and has been since we were first taken there long ago. And thankfully it has not changed in 40 years — except for the ER209 road.

Start this short circuit by leaving the **Fanal** FORESTRY HOUSE (**O**) off to your right and climbing the log steps seen ahead (with PR sign). Rising to a saddle, head right (the PR sign has fallen over here) on a wide but ferny and indistinct path that rounds the very edge of the northern escarpment with stupendous views. The path is wide enough to allay feelings of vertigo, but it's not a place to be in dense fog! The path then clears, narrows and continues in shade round the north side of **Pedreira**, a hill bearded in heath trees. At **20min** the path bends right at a PR sign for 'PAUL DA SERRA' (a corrugated iron hut is to the left) and you come to an unsigned junction. Turn left here past a tall CAIRN. In a few minutes you reach a track at a T-junction, where you turn left for 'FIO 0,3 KM'. This stony 4WD track passes some 'holiday huts' on the left — corrugated iron *palheiros* decorated with charm — before arriving at the *fio* (**❶**; **30min**), a disused goods hoist that used to plunge 1000m/3300ft down to Chão da Ribeira.

Return along the stony track past where you came in and keep ahead for 'PAUL DA SERRA 6,7 KM'. Ignore a track off right with a small cairn and continue — first detouring on the PR13 for 10-15 minutes return to another *miradouro* (**❷**) with much the same view as that from the *fio* — to a LARGE GRAZING AREA (**❸**), full of curious cows and swirling with seagulls. Now on a grassy track, ignore all crossing tracks as you round the south side of Pedreira, passing more of Fanal's *tils* and looking across the Ribeira da Janela Valley. Meeting a tarred road, go half right on another grassy track, back down to the **Fanal** FORESTRY HOUSE (**O**; **1h25min**).

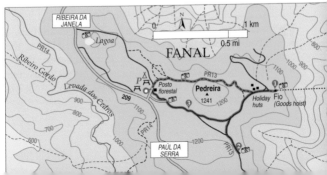

Walk 37: RABAÇAL'S LEVADAS

Map pages 124-125

Distance: 11.2km/7mi; 4h (but see Shorter walks below)

Grade: see 'The entire length' and Shorter walks

Equipment: stout shoes (boots preferable), fleece, long trousers, sunhat, windproof, whistle, rainhat, picnic, plastic bottle/water purifying tablets

How to get there and return: 🚗 car or *taxi* (from the Recta das Canhas; see Walk 35, page 122) to the large parking area on the ER105 above Rabaçal (32° 45.261'N, 17° 8.000'W; Car tour 5). Then 8-seater shuttle 🚐 to/from Rabaçal (the road is closed to private cars): runs about every 20min from 09.30-20.00 in summer, from 09.30-18.00 rest of the year, lunch break between 12.00-13.00; one way 3 €, return 5 €. Or walk the 2km down and back up (*tiring!*). Or park as for Alternative walk 1 below.

The entire length: ● ‼ moderate, with descents/re-ascents of 200m/650ft; you must be sure-footed and have a head for heights

Shorter walks

1 **Rabaçal — Risco — Rabaçal.** ● 2.5km/1.6mi; 50min. Easy (PR6.1). Access as above. Follow the main walk to Risco (❶) and back.

2 **Rabaçal — 25 Fontes — Rabaçal.** ● ‼ 6.4km/4mi; 1h40min. Easy, but you must be sure-footed and have a head for heights (*danger of vertigo*). Access as above. Follow the main walk for 9min, then turn left down the path (PR6) to the Levada das 25 Fontes. Do the main walk from the 25min-point to 25 Fontes (❸) and return the same way.

Alternative walks

1 **Rabaçal tunnel — Rabaçal levadas — Rabaçal tunnel.** ● ‼ 16km/10mi; 5h15min. Grade and equipment as main walk; take a *torch* as well. Access by 🚗. You may prefer this approach to Rabaçal if you don't want to wait for the shuttle bus or endure the tiring climb back up to the main road at the end of your walk. From the ER105 drive south on the cobbled ER211 and park about 2km downhill at a barbecue building on the right (🅲; 32° 45.240'N, 17° 8.966'W) — possibly burnt out; we had no time to check. From there follow the dirt track on the opposite side of the road to the Rabaçal tunnel (🅲; *P*37c; 10min) and go through it (20min). You emerge at a sun-trap on the Levada das 25 Fontes (🅑; *P*37b). Follow the levada for a minute, then turn right up steps to the Risco levada and Rabaçal (🅞). Do the main walk, but don't climb back up to Rabaçal; return to the sun-trap and go through the tunnel, back to your car.

2 **Rabaçal levadas — Rocha Vermelha tunnel — Loreto.** ● ‼ 18.7km/11.6mi; about 6h. Grade: moderate, but you must be sure-footed and have a head for heights (*danger of vertigo*). Equipment as main walk, *plus torch*. Access by 🚗 *taxi* (see Walk 35, page 122), then shuttle bus down to Rabaçal as for the main walk; return on 🚐 80, 115 or 142 from Loreto. Follow the main walk to the 3h20min-point; then, instead of climbing up to Rabaçal at ❻, continue through the Rocha Vermelha tunnel (20min), coming out in the fire-scorched Calheta Valley. Follow the levada to its tiny reservoir, then descend to Walk 35a at 🅓, to continue to Loreto (🅞; see page 123, just after the 2h50min-point).

Rabaçal is an enchanted fairyland of singing waterfalls, a favourite excursion spot for the islanders. Here at the head of Madeira's greatest valley, the Rabaçal house (*P*37a) lies dwarfed beneath emerald mountains. Three levadas converge here; each has its own 'personality', and this walk lets you make friends with all three.

Mossy trail beside the Levada do Risco

The walk begins at the **Rabaçal** houses (❍): follow signs to 'PR6.1, Risco' and 'PR 6, 25 Fontes', descending to the highest levada (1030m/3380ft), the **Levada do Risco**. Pass a fork to the Levada das 25 Fontes in **9min** and in **15min** ford a spillway created by a waterfall on the right. Around here the levada is flanked by an exceedingly beautiful mossy 'carpet' (see above), and the banks are built up high to cope with a great flow. At a fork, keep right on concrete to a view-point in a typical *caldeirão*, where the **Risco** WATERFALL (❶; **25min**; *P*37d) cascades into a pool from a height of 100m/325ft. A tunnel on the right disgorges even more water, drawn from below the Urze peak. From here you can see the levada continue around the head of the gorge to its source, but this dangerous route is closed to walkers. Look below, across the valley, to see a second channel cut into the mountainside: this is the 'middle' levada, leading to 25 Fontes ('25 Springs').

Now retrace your steps to the fork to 25 Fontes (**25min**). Turn right and descend stone steps to reach the **Levada das 25 Fontes** (altitude 960m/3150ft). Turn right and you will see the Risco waterfall again, from a lower level: in **55min** you come to the head of the gorge where it dives down. Then cross the bed of the **Ribeira Grande**, to meet a tiny WATER-HOUSE (❷): water is usually gushing out of its front door... From here on the levada channel is only 30cm/1ft wide in places, and there are drops at the left of up to 30m/100ft. But even without fencing we never found this levada vertiginous because, unlike most others, it is built up off the path, not sunk into it. The concrete edge of the levada is at waist level, and you can hold on to it for moral support if the drops worry you. It's cooling to run your hands in the water on a hot day.

In **1h15min** you pass the path down left to the Levada da Rocha Vermelha; ignore it for now. In about **1h25min**, in a tributary of the Cedros River, you reach a path leading up right (by a sluice) and at once you see the 'Vinte e Cinco' (25) Fontes — a semi-circular bowl into which tumble down many sparkling waterfalls (but, alas, no longer 25). It's a lovely place to paddle under ferns (❸; *P*37e).

Now return to the path passed 10 minutes earlier and turn down right to the Levada da Rocha Vermelha (❹; 1h 50min), at 850m/2790ft, the lowest of the Rabaçal levadas. A keepers' house sits below on your right. This levada is the newest of the three. Turn right on it, back up into the valley of the Ribeira dos Cedros. There are waterfalls left, right and centre! Take in the negative ions, then only continue if you are *absolutely sure-footed and vertigo-free*. You cross the Cedros ravine on the levada channel (covered with concrete slabs), and find a tunnel on your right: water is flowing in from mountains on the east side of the Seixal River, some 4km/2.5mi away. Turn left on the levada and follow it round the valley. Soon you're just opposite the *levadeiros'* house; some 200m/650ft directly above it you see the Rabaçal houses. Notice how the levada narrows beyond each tributary, as you head towards its source. In 2h25min you might like to take a break at a grassy promontory, from where there is a magnificent view of the Ribeira da Janela 200m/650ft below.

Time constraints will limit the distance you can walk on this levada; we stop after 2h40min, where the thick blue line ends on the map (❺)*. From here return the same way, enjoying grassy verges and the aroma of wild mint, open views and shady heath-tree bowers. You'll be back at the keepers' cottage in 3h10min. Stay on the levada, passing the path where you came down to it, and turning up into the Ribeira Grande. The Risco falls and the 25 Fontes Levada are visible ahead and above you. Across this wild gully yawns the Rocha Vermelha tunnel (Alternative walk 2); it disgorges in the Calheta Valley near the path of Walk 35a.

A bridge crosses the river, to the tunnel, but carry on past it, to the sluices and rock pools (3h20min), where you can take a break below the roaring (Risco) falls. Then walk back, cross the bridge, and turn *sharp left* up a STONE-LAID PATH (❻)**, to begin the climb back to Rabaçal. In 15 minutes you reach the Levada das 25 Fontes, where you turn right. Ten minutes later, just before a high tunnel (Walk 35a), steps on the left take you up to the picnic area at Rabaçal (O; 4h).

*About 15 minutes further on, you would find steps similar to those in the photograph on page 127 — but almost 300 of them! *Experts* might like to climb them (the descent is horrendously vertiginous) and pursue the levada to its source (another 50min; *not* shown on the map).

**If this path is still broken by landslides (as it was at press date), you will have to return via your descent path at ❹: this adds 35 minutes — or 45 minutes, if you go all the way to the tunnel on the 25 Fontes levada.

Walk 38: LEVADA DO ALECRIM

See map on pages 124-125   Distance: 7.2km/4.5mi; 1h50min

Grade: ● ¦ easy, but some of the paths are slippery and exposed; you must be sure-footed and have a head for heights (*possibility of vertigo*).

Equipment: stout shoes, picnic, water

How to get there and return: 🚗 car to the parking area on the ER105, at the top of the road to Rabaçal (32° 45.261'N, 17° 8.000'W; Car tour 5).

A short ramble along the Levada do Alecrím is easily combined with a day's touring on the Paúl da Serra. It takes its source in the Ribeira Grande, almost 300m/1000ft above the levadas followed in Walk 37. At 1300m/4265ft, this is the 'penthouse suite' of the Ribeira Grande levadas. But unlike the Walk 37 levadas, this one is twinned with the Levada do Paúl (Walk 35a) and flows into the reservoir on the ER105.

Start out at the car park (**a**): walk down the Rabaçal road for 120m/yds, then fork right on a path. This takes you to the wide **Levada do Alecrím**. A pretty amble brings you quickly to a small semi-circular reservoir, which may be brimming with tiny trout (**①**; **12min**; *P*38). Immediately past it, you cross the **Ribeira do Alecrím** (Rosemary River).

After a narrow, unprotected stretch with a sheer drop to the left (amply wide and quickly passed), you come to 50 shallow STEPS beside a water chute (like the one in the photograph at the top of page 127). These steps take you up to a viewpoint over the Ribeira da Janela and your starting point (**30min**) and then into the valley of the **Ribeira Grande**, from where you will have glimpses down to the three levadas followed in Walk 37.

You may notice a PATH (**②**) off left some 15 minutes past the steps: steep and narrow, it leads to the Lagoa do Vento, from where you could continue to Rabaçal. These paths are shown on our map, but the route — though perfectly viable as of press date — is not described here.

When you reach the SOURCE of the levada in the wide river bed (**③**; **55min**), a waterfall, rock pools and birdsong beckon you to bide a while. Then return the same way to the CAR PARK on the ER105 (**a**; **1h50min**).

Rock pools and waterfall in the bed of the Ribeira Grande

Walk 39: PICO RUIVO DO PAÚL

See map pages 124-125
Distance: 3.2km/2mi; 1h15min
Grade: ● easy climb/descent of 150m/500ft, but avoid the climb to the summit if there is any sign of mist descending; follow the levada to find your way back to your car.
Equipment: stout shoes, sunhat, picnic, water
How to get there and return: 🚗 car to the junction of the ER208 to Estanquinhos and ER105 to Bica da Cana, by a narrow levada (32° 45.873'N, 17° 4.919'W; Car tour 5)

Photograph: Pico Ruivo do Paúl, from the Estanquinhos/ Bica da Cana junction

By now it won't be a secret to you that the Paúl da Serra is our favourite place on Madeira — and with the new expressways you're there in a trice. Wonderful for picnicking and doing a few short walks on a 'lazy day'. This is another stunner!

Start out at the road JUNCTION (○): head north in the setting shown above, following the grassy banks beside the narrow blue ribbon of levada. The levada squiggles its way through a small birch wood (**10min**) and eventually crosses a track at the beautiful **Fonte Ruivas** picnic area (❶; *P39*). Just three minutes later, beyond a fenced water tank, you reach the levada's SOURCE (**20min**). Now just follow the trampled bracken up to the top of **Pico Ruivo do Paúl** (❷; **30min — 45min** on a hot day!). From here there is a wonderful view east, similar to that in the photograph on page 119.

From the summit head south towards 'Estanquinhos'. Keep right at a fork but, after crossing the Fontes Ruivas track, just make your way (no particular path) over the moorland, back to your car at the JUNCTION (○; **1h15min**).

View towards the Janela Valley from the water tank before it was encased in concrete and fenced off

Walk 40: FROM PRAZERES TO PAÚL DO MAR

Map pages 134-5, photo page 15 Distance: 3.7km/2.3mi; 1h35min
Grade: ● ‼ strenuous descent of about 550m/1800ft *in full sun*; you must be sure-footed and have a head for heights (*danger of vertigo*). *Avoid in damp weather,* when the path (PR19) is treacherously slippery. *Note:* To do the walk in reverse (easier on the knees and less vertiginous), walk through a narrow gap between houses, a few metres/yards uphill from the bar on the quay in Paúl do Mar, *before* the road bends left.
Equipment: stout shoes (walking boots preferable), sunhat, whistle, walking stick, picnic, water; extra fleece and windproof in cool weather
How to get there: 🚌 142 or 🚗 to Prazeres; by car, park at the Hotel Jardim Atlántico (32° 45.145'N, 17° 12.944'W; a detour on Car tour 6)
To return: 🚌 142 or 🚗 *taxi* from Paúl do Mar back to your car, or to the ER222 in time for the afternoon 🚌 80. Book a taxi at the office/bar by the church in Prazeres (there *are* taxis at Paúl do Mar, but they are sometimes away on day trips). Alternatively, climb back up to Prazeres (exhausting on a hot day), *if you are sure you can catch your return bus!*
Note: There are several other cliff-side routes on the southwest coast, but some are hard to locate and not well maintained. They are only recommended for very experienced walkers with a head for heights. These hikes are best suited to those staying at the Hotel Jardim Atlántico, where you can get a route map and advice on the viability of the paths.

T his is *the* five-star route on the southwest coast, a wonderfully exhilarating descent that spirals you down to photogenic Paúl do Mar. The focal points are the ochre-to-burgundy volcanic cliffs, a Swiss cheese landscape of caves and rivulets plastered with houseleeks and Pride of Madeira. You'll take photos galore!

Begin on the ER222 at **Prazeres** (○). Follow the signposted road through bucolic countryside to the HOTEL JARDIM ATLÁNTICO (❶; **30min**). At the far end of the hotel car park you'll see an information board and a finger post for the 'CAMINHO REAL DO PAÚL DO MAR' (PR19). Head down the concrete walkway with fine views over Jardim do Mar to the left and Paúl do Mar below. Soon steps take you down to an exquisite old cobbled trail. Some 10 minutes down, someone has thoughtfully placed a bench below pines, where you can sit and contemplate the fields and terraces below Maloeira on the plateau and Raposeira on the ridge beyond it (*P40*).

Soon the path goes into a roller-coaster descent and, just when you think you cannot stomach the pitch any longer, you're saved from the abyss by a zig or a zag. As you near the sea, look back into the great cleft where the Seca and Cova rivers come together and plummet 400m/1300ft in a graceful waterfall. After crossing a stone bridge over the **Ribeira Seca** in a delightful setting, descend for another five minutes, then turn down left to the tiny quay at **Paúl do Mar** (○; **1h35min**), where the falls crash onto the pebbly shore just behind the colourful fishing boats.

If you haven't arranged to be collected, walk along the coast to the nearby bar-restaurant, where they can call a taxi.

Walk 41: LEVADA CALHETA–PONTA DO PARGO

See also maps on pages 120 and 124-125, and the touring map

Grade: ● easy, if done in short sections — otherwise very long (●)

Distance: as individual walk suggestions

Equipment: stout shoes, sunhat, picnic, water

How to get there: 🚌 142 or 🚗 to Raposeira (32° 45.993'N, 17° 12.859'W)

To return: 🚌 back to your base or your car; see opposite

The Levada Calheta–Ponta do Pargo (see notes on page 123) is just perfect for strolling. As it contours along the sun-drenched plains above the coast, it gives you superb views up to the Paúl da Serra, where scudding clouds create an ever-changing mosaic on the hillsides. Gorgeous all year round, these walks are at their best in high summer, when the levada is full to brimming, and the agapanthus and hydrangeas are in bloom (in winter, the levada is sometimes empty). You stroll under pine and eucalyptus, by ferny glens and banks of lilies. While there is ample shade, sun protection is *essential*.

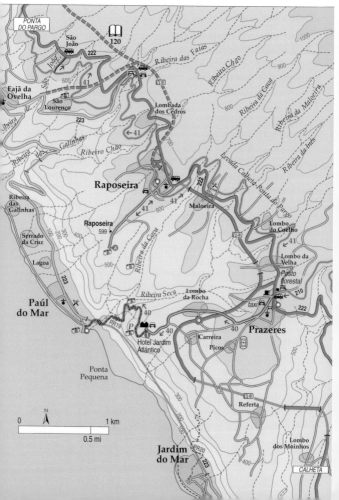

Walks 34 and 41: the Levada Calheta–Ponta do Pargo in July; you'll be a source of some curiosity to the locals!

Walk suggestions: Both of our suggestions begin below (just south of) Raposeira church (◐), but you can join the **Levada Calheta–Ponta do Pargo** at other convenient points. The *touring map* shows you at a glance where the levada crosses the road. If you are driving, there are several places to park along the quiet ER222, for example at the turn-off for Fajã da Ovelha. Perhaps combine your levada walk with a visit to the viewpoint over Paúl do Mar at Raposeira (❶; 2km return), or just amble down a grassy trail overlooking the lighthouse at Ponta do Pargo.

1   **Follow the levada east from Raposeira.** You can leave it for the ER222 at Prazeres (4.7km/3mi; 1h15min), Lombo dos Moinhos (10.2km/ 6.3mi; 2h35min), or the power station above Calheta (22km/13.7mi; 5h). Beyond the power station you could join Walk 35a and continue to Loreto (26.5km/16.5mi; 6h30min; map pages 124-125, notes page 125). This stretch is served by 🚌 80 and 142: *flag your bus down!*

2   **Head west from Raposeira** (maps below, page 121, touring map). You cross the road at Lombada dos Marinheiros, west of the Fajã da Ovelha turn-off (*only shown on the touring map;* 8km/5mi; 2h15min; 🚌 80, 142), but must descend to Ponta do Pargo (15km/9.3mi; 3h45min; 🚌 80, 142, 150). The levada ends above Cabo, on the route of Walk 34 (21.5km/13.3mi; 5h20min; 🚌 80, 142, 150: *flag them down!*).

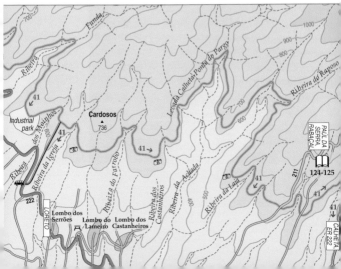

Walk 42: LEVADA DA CENTRAL DA RIBEIRA DA JANELA

Distance: 13.3km/8.2mi; 3h30min (9km/5.6mi; 2h30min if you turn back at the tunnel entrance)

Grade: ● ⁝ easy, but you must be sure-footed and have a head for heights (*possibility of vertigo*).

Equipment: stout shoes (walking boots preferable), long trousers, fleece, windproof, sunhat, rainhat, picnic, water, whistle, *torch for the tunnel*

How to get there and return: 🚗 car or *taxi* to the reservoir above Porto Moniz (32° 51.091'N, 17° 10.007'W). Ask a taxi driver for 'Lagoa'. By car, drive towards Santa on the EN101 and turn left for 'Lamaceiros' 3.5km up from the roundabout by the petrol station. Keep straight on past any forks. After 1km you pass to the left of the church/bus stop at Lamaceiros. When the road bends right after a further 300m, go straight ahead and park at the recreation area (with café) by the levada. Or 🚌 80 or 150 to/from the church at Lamaceiros (ⓐ) and walk on to the levada.

Short walk: to the second filtration point and back. 3.5km/2.2mi; 1h. Easy. Follow the main walk for 30min and return the same way.

From the western flanks of the great Janela Valley you look across to the stupendous array of tiny terraces tumbling helter-skelter from Ribeira da Janela down to the river far below. Then you leave the cultivation behind, for ferny glens, mossy cliffs and primeval woodlands.

Start out at the RESERVOIR IN THE RECREATION AREA (**○**) and follow the wide **Levada da Central da Ribeira da Janela** (inaugurated 1965) past a picnic table (**3min**; *P*42) and a

In about 30 minutes the levada widens by a second filtration point. The path is lined with fruit trees intertwined with passion flowers. This is an especially beautiful picnic spot (a second setting for Picnic 42). Further along you'll walk beneath beech trees and indigenous laurels and skirt high escarpments bearded with a great variety of ferns.

then a wide filtration point. Huge bushes of fennel, apple and fig trees, and garlands of passion flowers herald the next filtration tank (**❶**; **30min**; *P*42). Five minutes later, notice the cables used for moving supplies between the water-course and the valley floor. Down by the river one of the most impressive expanses of terracing on the island stretches out below you.

Within **45min** the sure of foot will reach a ferny glen in the upper reaches of the **Ribeira da Cova Negra**. Soon you skirt a rock wall pouring with rainwater. In **1h** you are looking straight up the Janela Valley; with binoculars you can easily see the Rabaçal houses from here (Walks 35 and 37). It takes 10 minutes to go through the TUNNEL met in a tributary of the **Ribeira da Quebrada** (**❷**; **1h15min**). You emerge in a typical *caldeirão* with waterfall. Beyond a shorter TUNNEL, continue 15 minutes to a WATERHOUSE (**❸**; **1h45min**), before turning back* to catch the bus or collect your car by the RESERVOIR (**❶**; **3h30min**).

*There are six more tunnels beyond this waterhouse, one of which takes about 30 minutes. It is possible for *experts* to follow the levada to a keepers' house and then the source (about 2h from here; strong torch and raingear needed ... but you will probably get soaked anyway). At time of writing all the sheer drops were protected with railings or fences. From the keepers' house a steep path, then a track climbs 850m/2800ft (7km/ 4.3mi; about 3h) to Fonte do Bispo. This route is *not* shown on any of our maps. Arrange to be met on the ER105 at the 'Galhano' signpost, opposite Fonte do Bispo (Car tour 5).

BUS TIMETABLES

Below is a list of destinations serving the walks in this book. Numbers following place names are *bus numbers;* they are arranged below in numerical order. *But all orange 'town' buses are on page 142.* See page 9 for more bus information and websites and pages 10-11 for bus departure points. Note that where intermediate times are shown, they are **approximate: arrive early! No buses run on Christmas day.**

Achadinha 111
Águas Mansas 60, 77, 110
Arco de São Jorge 6, 103, 132
Assomada 2, 20, 23, 53, 78, 113, 208
Babosas *town* 🚐 22
Barreira *town* 🚐 10A
Boa Morte 127, 148
Boaventura 6
Boqueirão 60, 110
Cabo Girão 154
Camacha 77, 129
Campanário 6, 7, 115, 123, 139, 142, 148
Canhas 115, 142
Caniçal 113
Corticeiras 96
Cruz 53, 78
Cruzinhas 56, 103, 138
Curral das Freiras 81
Curral dos Romeiros *town* 🚐 29
Eira do Serrado 81
Encumeada 6
Estreito de C.d. Lobos 3, 6, 7,

96, 115, 123, 139, 142, 148, 154
Faial 53, 56, 78, 103, 138
Fontes 127, 148
Formiga 115, 142
Ilha de São Jorge 103, 132, 138
Jardim Botânico *town* 🚐 29, 30, 31
Lamaceiros 80, 139, 150
Lombo Grande 60
Loreto 115, 142
Machico 20, 23, 53, 56, 78, 113, 208
Maroços 156, 208
Madeira Shopping *town* 🚐 8, 8a, 16, 150
Monte 56, 103, 138, *town* 🚐 20, 21
Nogueira 110, 114
Palheiro Ferreiro 77, 129, *town* 🚐 36, 36A, 37, 47
Paúl do Mar 80, 115
Pico do Facho (turn-off to) 113
Poiso 56, 103, 138

Ponta do Pargo 80, 142
Ponta do Sol 80 (direct); or 115, 142 (via the ER222)
Portela 53, 78
Porto da Cruz 53, 56, 78, 103, 138, 208
Porto Moniz 80, 139, 150
Prazeres 80, 142
Raposeira 80, 142
Ribeira Brava 6, 7, 80, 115, 127, 139, 142
Ribeira Seca 113
Ribeirinha 111
Ribeiro Frio 56, 103, 138
Santa 80, 139, 150
Santana 56, 103, 132, 138
Santo da Serra 20, 77, 78
São João Latrão *town* 🚐 47
São Jorge 103, 132, 138
São Lourenço Point 113
São Vicente 6, 139, 150
Sítio Quatro Estradas 77
Stadium *town* 🚐 45
Vale Paraíso 77, 129

2 Funchal • Assomada (journey time 40min)
Departs Funchal: 07.30, 08.20+, 08.30§, 09.15+, 10.00, 11.00, 11.35+, 11.45▢, 12.00•, 12.10+, 13.00, 14.00*, 15.00, 16.00*, 16.30•, 17.00*, 17.45*, 18.00•, 18.45*, 19.00•, 19.30*, 20.15*, 20.30•, 21.00*, 22.30, 23.45

Departs Assomada: 06.45•, 07.00*, 07.30*, 08.10*, 08.30•, 09.10+, 09.30§, 09.55+, 11.00, 11.40* 12.00•, 12.15+, 12.25▢, 13.00+, 13.30•, 13.45*, 14.40*, 14.45•, 15.40, 16.40*, 17.00+, 17.45, 18.30*, 19.00•, 19.30*, 21.10+, 21.30§, 21.45+, 23.10

3 Funchal • Estreito de Câmara de Lobos (journey time 45min)
Departs Funchal: 08.45§, 10.30+, 11.45#, 11.55+, 12.45, 14.05•, 14.45§, 15.00+, 15.45§, 16.10+, 16.40+⤢, 16.45▢, 17.00+, 17.30▢, 18.15+, 18.45▢, 19.15+, 19.45§

Departs Estreito (a): 06.50+, 07.05▢, 07.20+, 08.05+, 08.15+, 08.20▢, 08.50+, 09.45§, 10.05+, 11.35+, 13.05§, 13.40§, 14.00+, 15.05+, 15.45§, 16.20+, 16.45§, 17.25+, 17.45▢, 18.05+, 20.40§, 22.35, 24.00

6 Funchal • Arco de São Jorge (via Estreito, Campanário, Ribeira Brava, São Vicente)

Funchal	07.35			13.35*(b)		15.30•⤢ 17.35(b)	
Ribeira Brava	08.50			14.50*		16.45•⤢ 18.50	
Encumeada	09.30			15.30*		00.00 19.30	
São Vicente	09.50	11.00+	13.15+	15.30+	15.50*	17.00+¶ 17.15•⤢ 19.50	
P. Delgada	10.05	11.15+	13.30+	15.50+¶	16.05*	17.15+¶ 17.30•⤢ 20.05	
Boaventura	10.45	11.25+	13.40+	16.00+¶	16.45*	17.20+¶ 17.35•⤢ 21.00	
Arco S. Jorge	11.30	11.45+				17.50+¶ 17.50•⤢ 21.20	

Arco S. Jorge		06.40⤢		11.50+	14.30		17.50•⤢ 21.20	
Boaventura	05.50+⤢ 06.55⤢	09.15+	12.15+	14.45	17.30▢	18.05•⤢ 21.35	
P. Delgada	06.20+⤢ 07.25⤢	09.30+	12.45+	15.15	17.40▢	18.15•⤢ 21.45(c)	
S. Vicente	06.35+⤢ 08.00⤢	09.45+	13.00+	15.30	17.50▢	18.25•⤢ 21.55(c)	
Encumeada	00.00 00.00			16.00		00.00	
Ribeira Brava	07.30+⤢ 08.40⤢			16.30		19.00•⤢	
Funchal	08.30+⤢ 09.20⤢			17.40		20.10•⤢	

(a) Departures do not *start* from Estreito; departure times have been estimated and may be as much as 15min *later;* (b) only to Boaventura; (c) Fri/Sat terminates at São Vicente; *see other symbol codes opposite.*

7 Funchal • Ribeira Brava (journey time 1h30min)

Departs Funchal: 06.35*, 07.30+ꚾ, 07.55+ꚾ, 09.00+ꚾ, 09.30+, 10.05•, 10.15•ꚾ, 11.00*ꚾ, 12.05•, 13.30•, 14.00*ꚾ, 15.30*, 16.55+ꚾ, 17.00§, 18.00+ꚾ, 18.15+ꚾ, 20.15, 21.15+, 22.15, 23.30

Departs Ribeira Brava: 06.05, 07.00+§, 07.15+ꚾ, 07.30+ꚾ, 08.05*, 08.15+ꚾ, 08.45+ꚾ, 09.00+ꚾ, 09.05□ꚾ, 10.10+ꚾ, 11.00*, 11.45•, 12.00+ꚾ, 12.35+, 13.35•, 14.30+ꚾ, 15.30+ꚾ, 17.30*, 18.35, 19.00ꚾ, 22.10

20 Funchal • Machico • Santo da Serra (via Gaula and Machico)

Funchal	07.15*	09.30+	12.40	16.30+	19.15+	20.45+
Machico	08.00*	10.20+	13.25	17.25+	19.55+	21.30+
Santo da Serra *(arrives)*	08.35*	10.55+	14.05	18.25+	20.30+	22.00+

Santo da Serra *(departs)*	06.30	08.00*	09.45*	12.20+	14.00□	14.45+	16.15•
Machico	07.00	08.45*	10.25*	12.55+	14.30□	15.20+	17.00•
Funchal	07.45	09.30*	11.15*	13.45+	15.20□	16.15+	17.45•

23 Funchal • Machico (journey time 35min direct express)

Departs Funchal: 07.00+, 08.00+, 11.30+ until 15.30+ hourly at 30min past the hour, then half-hourly until 19.30+

Departs Machico: 06.30+ until 10.00+ half-hourly, then 11.30+, 12.30+, 13.30+, and 14.00+ until 17.30+ half-hourly; then 18.45+

53 Funchal • ✈ • Machico • Ribeira de Machico • Portela • Porto da Cruz • Faial

Funchal		10.00*	13.15*			16.30+	17.20*	18.15•	18.20+
Machico	09.00*	10.50*	14.05*	14.30•	15.30+	17.10+	18.00*	19.00•	19.00+
Portela	09.25*	11.15*	14.20*	14.50•	15.50+	17.30+	18.25*	19.25•	19.25+
Pto Cruz	09.35*	11.30*	14.35*	15.05•	16.20+	17.45+	19.35*	19.35•	19.35+
Faial *(arr)*	09.45*	11.45*	14.45*	15.15•		17.55+	18.45*	19.45•	19.45+

Faial *(dep)*	06.45+	07.40+		10.15	13.00+	13.30•	15.30+	17.15*	18.20+
Pto Cruz	07.05	08.05+	08.00	10.25	13.10+	13.40•	15.40*	17.25*	18.35+
Portela	07.20	08.20+	08.15	10.40	13.25+	13.55•	15.55*	17.40*	18.50+
Machico	07.40	08.40+	08.35	11.00	13.50•	14.30•	16.30*	18.00*	19.15+
Funchal	08.30	09.30+	09.25	12.00	14.45•	15.20•	17.20*	18.45*	20.05+

56 Funchal • Faial • Santana (routing varies; see a-d)

Funchal	08.10+a	10.00*a	10.30•a	12.20+b	14.00□b/d	17.05+b/d
Faial	09.20+a	11.20*a	11.35•a	13.35+b	15.30□b/d	18.25+b/d
Santana	10.00+a	11.30*a	12.00•a	13.50+b	~~00.00~~	~~00.00~~

Santana		11.00*a	12.00□b	13.00+b	15.30#b
Faial	06.30*b/d	11.10+a	12.15□b	13.30+b	15.45#b
Funchal	07.40*b/d	12.50+a	13.30□b	14.40+b	17.10#b

a: northbound via Poiso, Ribeira Frio, São Roque; southbound via São Roque, Ribeira Frio, Poiso
b: northbound via Porto da Cruz *(tunnel)*, São Roque, Cruzinhas; southbound via Cruzinhas, São Roque, Porto da Cruz *(tunnel)*
c: via Poiso, Ribeira Frio, Cruzinhas; d: terminates/begins at Faial

60 Funchal • Boqueirão (via Gaula; journey time 1h)

Departs Funchal: 11.00#, 13.30*, 17.00+, 18.25+, 19.15#, 20.30+
Buses pass Gaula approx. 10min and Lombo Grande 5min before Boqueirão.

Departs Boqueirão: 07.30*, 08.20+, 11.30+, 12.45+, 13.05#, 13.45+, 15.00+, 17.00§
Buses pass Lombo Grande approx. 5min and Gaula 10min after Boqueirão.

77 Funchal • Santo da Serra (via Camacha)

Funchal	07.35*	08.30•	10.30	14.00	16.30	18.00*	19.15#
Camacha	08.10*	09.10•	11.10	14.40	17.10	18.40*	19.55#
Sítio Quatro Estradas	08.40*	09.40•	11.40	15.10	17.40	19.10*	20.25#
Santo da Serra *(arrives)*	08.50*	09.50•	11.50	15.20	17.50	19.20*	20.35#

Santo da Serra *(departs)*	06.30	09.00*	09.50•	12.00#	16.15	18.00	20.30+
Sítio Quatro Estradas	06.35	09.05*	09.55•	12.05#	16.20	18.05	20.35+
Camacha	07.10	09.40*	10.30•	12.40#	16.55	18.40	21.10+
Funchal	07.50	10.20*	11.10•	13.20#	17.35	19.20	21.50+

~~00.00~~ no service; +Mon-Fri; *not on 31 Dec or 1 Jan; □only Saturdays; *not Sundays or holidays; ‡only Mon/Wed/Fri; •only Sundays/holidays; ••only Sundays; ✝not Sundays or the first Saturday in Sept.; #not Saturdays; §Sat/Sun/holidays only; ¶in the school season only; ✤ except 1, 6 Jan, 25, 26 Dec, via the coastal road and Ponta do Sol; **only on holidays; ▲Mondays to Saturdays, also holidays; ++Tue, Wed, Thur, Fri only; ꚾ via the Via Rápida and/or the Encumeada Tunnel

78 Funchal • Machico • Faial (via Santo da Serra and Portela); routing varies; see a-d

Funchal	08.00•d	12.40**a		16.30□d	Faial	06.45▲	17.30•
Machico	08.50•a	13.25**a	17.00+c	17.15□d	Machico	07.45▲	18.30•
Faial (arr)	09.40•d		18.00+c	18.30□d	Funchal (arr)	08.35▲	19.30•

a: via Gaula; b: via the airport; terminates at Porto da Cruz (14.15); c: from Machico; terminates at Porto da Cruz; d: via Gaula and the airport

80 Funchal • Porto Moniz (via Ponta do Pargo, Paúl do Mar, Santa and Lamaceiros

Funchal (departs) 10.00+ ⪡ ; Ribeira Brava 11.00+ (10min stop)+; Calheta 11.25 (10min stop)+; Paúl do Mar 12.00+; Ponta do Pargo 12.40+; Santa 13.10+; Porto Moniz 13.15+

Funchal (departs) 14.35*; Ribeira Brava 16.00 (10min stop)*; Calheta 17.10 (10min stop)*; Ponta do Pargo 17.45*; Santa 18.15*; Porto Moniz 18.30*

Porto Moniz (departs) 16.00; Santa 16.15; Ponta do Pargo 16.45; Calheta 17.35 (10min stop); Ponta do Sol; Ribeira Brava 19.00 ⪡ (10min stop); Funchal 19.30

81 Funchal • Curral das Freiras (some journeys via the Eira do Serrado; journey time 45min)

Departs Funchal: 06.40•, 06.55+, 07.40*, 08.25+, 08.45□ ᴱˢ, 09.00#ᴱˢ, 10.00*ᴱˢ, 11.00+ᴱˢ, 11.30□ᴱˢ, 11.40•ᴱˢ, 12.15+, 13.15, 15.00+, 16.30, 17.30+, 18.30+, 19.30#, 19.30□ᴱˢ, 20.30+, 21.45, 23.45
Departs Curral (from Lombo Chão terminus): 07.30*, 07.40•, 08.45*, 09.30+, 10.00□, 10.10+, 10.30•, 11.10+ᴱˢ, 12.00□, 12.15+, 12.50□ᴱˢ, 16.15+ᴱˢ, 17.45, 19.30+, 20.30#•, 20.50+, 22.45

96 Funchal • Jardim da Serra/Corrida (via Estreito de Câmara de Lobos; journey time 1h)

Departs Funchal: 07.00•, 07.30+, 08.05ᶜ, 09.05+, 09.15□•, 09.45+ᶜ, 10.45*, 12.15+*ᶜ, 13.05*, 14.15+, 15.05, 16.05, 16.40+ᶜ, 17.15+ᶜ, 17.30, 18.30+, 18.35ᶜ, 19.15+ᶜ, 19.50§, 20.15+, 21.15
Departs Jardim da Serra: 06.30, 06.45*, 07.00+, 08.00, 08.45+, 09.00□, 10.15, 11.00+ᶜ, 12.30□, 12.45+, 13.30+ᶜ, 14.00□, 14.30+, 15.30+, 16.05§, 16.30+, 17.05§ᶜ, 17.40+ᶜ, 18.00+, 18.35§, 20.00

103 Funchal • Santana • Arco de São Jorge (routing varies; see a-d below)

Funchal	07.30+a	07.30§b	13.30+b	13.30□a	16.00*a/c	18.00+a	18.00§b
Pto da Cruz	08.10+a	00.00	00.00	14.15□a	16.40*a/c	18.45+a	00.00
Ribeiro Frio	00.00	08.15§b	14.15+b	00.00	00.00	00.00	18.50§b
Santana	09.30+a	09.15§b	15.05+b	14.40□a	17.10*a/c	19.05+a	19.40§b
Arco	10.50+a	10.25§b	15.55+b	15.30□a	18.00*a/c	20.05+a	20.40§b
Arco	06.00□b	06.20+a	07.20*a	07.20•b	12.30*a	16.30b/d	
Santana	06.45□b	07.05+a	08.30*a	08.25•b	13.25*a	17.30b/d	
Ribeiro Frio	07.30□b	00.00	00.00	09.10•b	00.00	18.35b/d	
Pto da Cruz	00.00	07.25+a	09.05*a	00.00	13.45*a	00.00	
Funchal	08.30□b	08.10+a	09.50*a	10.05•b	14.30*a	19.20b/d	

a: northbound via Porto da Cruz (tunnel), Cruzinhas, Ilha; southbound via Faial and Porto da Cruz (tunnel), b: northbound via Ribeiro Frio, Ilha; southbound via Cruzinhas and Ribeiro Frio
c: does not call at Ilha de São Jorge; d: calls at Ilha de São Jorge

110 Funchal • Boqueirão (via Caniço and Nogueira; journey time 40min)

Departs Funchal: 09.15+ˣ, 09.45+ˣ, 12.30*, 15.30+, 16.00□, 16.15+, 18.30#
Departs Boqueirão: 08.45#, 10.00+ˣ, 10.30+ˣ, 13.45*, 17.00+ˣ

111 Funchal • Achadinha (via Ribeirinha; journey time 1h)

Departs Funchal: 08.30+, 10.15*, 13.00, 15.45+, 18.15+, 19.05+, 19.45+
Departs Achadinha: 06.30+, 07.10+, 08.15+, 09.15+, 11.00+, 13.45, 16.30+

113 Funchal • Caniçal (via ✦ and Machico; journey time 1h10min)

Departs Funchal: 07.00+, 07.30•, 08.00+, 08.30*ˢᴸ, 09.00#ˢᴸ, 11.15*ˢᴸ, 12.15ˢᴸ, 13.30•ˢᴸ, 13.45+ᴿˢ, 14.30*ˢᴸ, 15.00+, 15.00•ˢᴸ, 15.30+ˢᴸ, 15.45•ᴿˢ, 16.30•ˢᴸ, 17.15*, 18.15+*ˢᴸ, 19.00#, 19.30+, 19.45□, 20.00+ᴿˢ, 22.30#ᴿˢ

Departs Caniçal: 05.45*, 06.45, 07.30*, 08.00+, 08.30+, 09.30, 10.20*ˢᴸ, 11.40*ˢᴸ, 11.55•*ˢᴸ, 12.55+ˢᴸ, 13.00□ˢᴸ, 13.55+ˢᴸ, 14.00§ˢᴸ, 15.00+ˢᴸ, 17.00ˢᴸ, 18.00*ˢᴸ, 19.00•ˢᴸ, 19.40*ˢᴸ, 21.00§

114 Funchal • Nogueira (via Caniço; journey time approximately 45min)

Departs Funchal: 06.30, 07.35, 08.45§, 09.30+, 10.00§, 11.15, 13.45*, 14.30, 16.30, 17.15+, 17.40, 18.25+, 18.50, 19.20*, 20.30, 22.00, 22.45+, 23.30, 00.15+
Departs Nogueira: 06.00, 07.00, 07.30+, 08.00+, 08.15, 09.25§, 10.15+, 10.40§, 11.55, 14.30*, 15.15, 17.15, 18.00+, 18.20, 19.30, 21.15, 22.15+, 22.45, 23.30+

115 Funchal • Estreito da Calheta • Paúl do Mar (journey time 2h50min)

Departs Funchal 16.05* (terminates at Estreito da Calheta on Saturdays), 19.05+
Departs Paul do Mar 05.45+, 11.40+ (from Prazeres, not Paúl do Mar)

ˢᴸgoes on to/returns from São Lourenço Point; ᶜgoes on to/returns from Corrida; ᴿˢterminates at/returns from Ribeira Sêca; ᴱˢvia the Eira do Serrado; ˣonly to Camacha. **See other symbol codes opposite.**

123 Funchal • Campanário (journey time 1h05min)
Departs Funchal: 11.30+, 13.00+, 18.00#; *Departs Campanário:* 12.40+, 14.30+

127 Ribeira Brava • Boa Morte (journey time 40min) • Fontes (journey time 55min)
Departs Ribeira Brava: 07.50+, 08.45§, 11.10*, 13.20+   *Departs Fontes:* 08.50+
The buses at 08.45 and 11.10 go only to Boa Morte; return from Boa Morte at 09.10, 11.35.

129 Funchal • Camacha (journey time 35min)
Departs Funchal: 08.00+, 08.15□, 09.00, 10.00, 11.00, 11.40+, 11.45§, 12.15+, 12.30•, 13.00+, 13.25□, 13.30#, 14.30, 15.30, 17.00, 17.30*, 18.00#, 18.15+, 18.30*, 18.40+¶, 18.50+, 19.00, 19.30+, 19.50□, 20.00#, 20.25□, 20.30•, 22.00, 22.30

Departs Camacha: 06.45□, 07.00#, 07.05+, 07.15+, 07.30+, 08.05□, 08.15#, 08.45*, 09.45, 10.45, 11.45, 12.25*, 13.00+, 13.15§, 13.45+, 14.15, 15.15, 16.15, 17.40, 18.15*, 18.45#, 19.15*, 19.45, 21.00§, 22.45

132 Santana • Arco de São Jorge (journey time approximately 55min)
Departs Santana: 06.00+; *Departs Arco:* 18.00+

138 Funchal • Cabanas, São Jorge (routing varies; see a–d below)
Departs Funchal: 11.30+a/d, 16.30•a/c, 18.00+b/c, 19.10+a/c
Departs Cabanas: 05.20+b/c/d, 06.40+b (begins at Santana), 09.45•a/c, 10.00+a
a: northbound via Porto da Cruz *(tunnel)* and Faial; southbound via Faial and Porto da Cruz *(tunnel)*
b: northbound via Ribeiro Frio and Faial; southbound via Faial and Ribeiro Frio
c: calls at Cruzinhas; d) calls at Ilha de São Jorge
For times to intermediate destinations such as Ribeiro Frio compare bus 103.

139 Funchal • Porto Moniz and Santa (via Encumeada tunnel; journey time 3h)
Departs Funchal 09.00 ⋝ (only to Porto Moniz, then departs for Santa at 16.00), 17.35*a
Departs Santa 05.45*+, 16.45+ ⋝ (from Porto Moniz, not Santa; journey time only 1h45min!)
a: on Saturdays uses the old road over Encumeada Pass; on Mon, Wed, Fri calls at Ribeira da Janela (Tue, Thur and Sat takes tunnel straight from Seixal to Porto Moniz)

142 Funchal • Ponta do Pargo (journey time 3h45min)
Departs Funchal: 08.05a, 12.00+ ⋝ , 16.00•, 17.35*
Departs Ponta do Pargo: 05.30+, 06.30, 07.30•+, 13.45+ (via Paul do Mar), 14.30 ⋝
a: arrives Ribeira Brava 09.30, Formiga 10.10, Recta das Canhas 10.30, Prazeres 11.10, Ponta do Pargo 12.00; the bus departing Ponta do Pargo at 14.35 passes Prazeres at about 15.05. *All times are approximate!*

148 Funchal • Boa Morte (journey time 1h20min)
Departs Funchal: 13.05*, 18.10*; *Departs Boa Morte:* 06.50*, 14.30*

150 São Vicente • Santa (journey time 45min)
Departs São Vicente: 10.25■, 16.10■; *Departs Santa:* 06.30■, 14.00■

154 Funchal • Cabo Girão (journey time 1h)
Departs Funchal: 08.50•, 10.35□, 11.30+, 17.00*, 19.00*
Departs Cabo Girão: 11.50§, 12.50+, 18.00+

208 (or 156; see note below) Funchal • Machico • Maroços • Porto da Cruz • (Moinhos, Faial)

Funchal	08.00*a	10.30	11.45▲	13.45□	14.30+	15.00□a	16.00*
Machico	08.50*a	11.20	12.35▲	14.35□	15.05+	15.45□a	16.50*
Maroços	09.05*a	11.40	12.50▲	14.50□	15.15+	16.00□a	17.05*
Pto da Cruz	00.00	11.50	13.00+	15.00□	15.25+	00.00	17.20*
Moinhos	00.00	00.00	00.00	00.00	15.35+	00.00	17.30*
Moinhos	07.15•	09.00+	11.00+	00.00	00.00	00.00	00.00
Pto da Cruz	07.25•	09.10+	11.10+	12.00b	13.00+	14.00+¶	15.00□
Maroços	07.35•	09.20+	00.00	12.30b	13.40+	14.10+¶	15.30□
Machico	07.45•	09.30+	11.30+	12.45b	13.55+	14.30+¶	15.45□
Funchal	08.35•	10.05+	12.05+	13.35b	14.40+	15.10+¶	16.45□

Buses labelled 'a' are numbered 156 and terminate about 30m/100ft below the Levada do Caniçal in the centre of Maroços; the 208 buses continue east uphill en route to the expressway towards Porto da Cruz, passing the bar A Calçadinha opposite the start of the levada (see map on pages 80-81). Several 156 buses (not shown here) run between Machico and Maroços — details from the Machico tourist office or the SAM website.

00.00 no service; +Mon-Fri; ■not on 26, 31 Dec, 1 Jan or Good Friday; □only Saturdays; *not Sundays or holidays; ‡only Mon/ Wed/Fri; •only Sundays/holidays; ••only Sundays; †not Sundays or the first Saturday in Sept.; #not Saturdays; §Sat/Sun/holidays only; ¶in the school season only; ✤except 1, 6 Jan, 25, 26 Dec, via the coastal road and Ponta do Sol; **only on holidays; ▲Mondays to Saturdays, also holidays; ++Tue, Wed, Thur, Fri only; ⋝ via the Via Rapida and/or the Encumeada Tunnel

HORARIOS DO FUNCHAL (operators of the orange town buses)

A helpful map for tourists, showing all town bus routes, is posted at the Horarios office in Anadia Shopping (11 on the town plan) and their information kiosks on the Avenida do Mar (see *i* symbol on the town plan on pages 10-11). Since their website and android information is so efficient, Horarios no longer go to the expense of providing printed maps and time-tables. Instead, these are posted at bus stops (note down the times of interest or, better still, take a picture on your smartphone!) and their principal information kiosk just east of the Electricity Museum (no 33 on the plan). Weekly tourist passes are available (21.85 € at time of writing). Otherwise there are 1-day passes (4.60 €), 3-day passes (11.80 €), or 5-day passes (16.20 €). You can also pay the driver as you board, but it's more expensive (1.95 € at time of writing; keep small notes and coins handy).

It is not possible to list all departure times in the limited space below; where specific services *are* shown, only the departure times you are most likely to use are listed. Note also that these departure times change frequently; re-check departure times at the bus shelters shown on the town plan. ***Better still, download their map of routes and all the timetables you require in advance of your visit;*** the Horarios interactive website (www.horariosdofunchal.pt) is super-efficient and even shows every bus stop on each route!

1 Lombada ('Ponta da Laranjeira' bus; journey time approx. 30min) ■

2 Quebradas ('Papagaio Verde' bus; journey time approx. 30min) ■

3 Lombada (journey time approx 30min) ■

4 Amparo (journey time approx. 20min)
Services too numerous to list; generally every 20 minutes (hourly on weekends).

6 Lido (journey time approx. 20min) ■
Restricted Sunday service, except in summer. Check at the bus stop!

8 Madeira Shopping (journey time approx. 30min) ■

10A Chamorra (Barreira) (journey time approx. 45min)
Departs Funchal: 07.20*, 07.30+, 07.50*, 08.00, 08.25+, 08.55, 10.00, 10.45+, 11.00, 11.40+ 12.15, 12.35, 12.55+, 13.05 (many more departures in the afternoon)
Departs Barreira: 12.05+, 12.45, 13.10+, 13.25, 13.45+, 14.00+, 14.30, 15.30, 16.30, 17.00+ 17.20+, 17.30, 18.05+, 18.25 (many more departures in the morning, and evening until 23.40)

16 Madeira Shopping (journey time approx. 30min)* ■

20, 21 Monte (journey time approx. 30min) ■ see also bus 22
You can walk between Monte and Babosas in 10 minutes, past the Monte Palace Gardens and cable car station

22 Babosas (journey time approx. 30min) ■ see also buses 20, 21
You can walk between Monte and Babosas in 10 minutes, past the Monte Palace Gardens and cable car station

29 Curral dos Romeiros (via the Jardim Botânico; journey time approx. 30min)
Departs Funchal: 07.00*, 07.20*, 07.45, 08.20*, 08.40•, 08.50*, 10.00, 10.30*, 11.00, 12.05+ 12.20•, 12.35, 13.05, 13.30*, 15.30*, 15.45•, 17.35+, 18.00+, 18.35, 19.00+, 19.35
Departs Curral dos Romeiros: 08.10, 08.45*, 09.05•, 09.15*, 10.35•, 11.05*, 11.30, 12.40#, 13.05* 13.35, 14.05*, 14.30•, 16.05, 18.10*, 18.55•, 19.05, 19.25+, 20.00, 21.00

30 Jardim Botânico ('Largo do Miranda' bus; journey time approx. 15min)
Hourly or every two hours every day of the week.

31 Jardim Botânico (journey time approx. 15min) ■

36 Palheiro Ferreiro ('Lombo da Quinta' bus; journey time approx. 25min) ■
This bus terminates on the northeast side of the Palheiro Gardens.

36A Palheiro Ferreiro (journey time approx. 25min) ■
This bus passes to the east of the Palheiro Gardens, crosses the Levada dos Tornos and terminates just north of the stadium at Palheiro Ferreiro.

37 Palheiro Ferreiro (journey time approx. 25min)
Departs Funchal: 07.55+, 09.00+, 12.00, 13.10, 16.45, 17.30+, 18.10, 19.20
Departs Palheiro Ferreiro: 12.35, 13.40, 17.15§, 17.40+, 18.20+, 18.40, 19.20+, 19.50
Stops at the entrance to the Palheiro Gardens; also at the Levada dos Tornos on the ER205.

45 Funchal • Levada dos Piornais ('Nazaré' bus; journey time approx 10min) ■

47 São João Latrão (journey time approx. 25min) ■

■Services too numerous to list and growing all the time; please consult the Horarios website; *no Sundays or holidays; #not Saturdays; +Mon-Fri; §Sat/Sun/holidays only; •Sundays only

● Index

Pronunciation/translation of some index entries

achada (ah-scháh-dah) small plateau
água (áh-gwah) water
arco (áhr-koo) arc or curving mountain ridge
baía (bah-ée-ah) bay
baixo (bíe-joo) low
balcões (bahl-kóyngs) balconies
bica (bée-kah) small spring
boca (bóe-kah) mountain pass (literally 'mouth')
brava (bráh-vah) wild
cabo (káh-boo) cape
caldeirão (kahl-day-roúngh) cauldron, crater, basin
calheta (kahl-yáy-tah) creek
câmara (káh-mah-rah) chamber
caminho (kah-méen-yoo) way, path, road
campo (káhm-poo) plain
caniço (kah-née-soo) reed
chão (shoúng) flat place
choupana (show-páh-nah) cottage
corticeiras (kohr-tee-sáy-rash) small cork trees
cova (kóh-vah) pit, cave
cruz (krúj) cross
cruzinhas (kru-zéen-yash) crossroads
curral (koo-ráhl) corral

dentro (déhn-troo) inside
eira (éye-rah) threshing floor
encumeada (in-koo-mee-áh-dah) summit with fine views
estanquinhos (esh-tahn-kéen-yosh) small ponds
estreito (esh-tráy-too) the straits above
faial (fie-áhl) beech grove
fajã (fah-jáh) small landslide
folhadal (fohl-yah-dáhl) lily-of-the-valley tree grove
fonte (fóhnt) spring
fora (fóh-rah) outside
janela (jha-náy-lah) window
jardim (jahr-déengh) garden
lamaceiros (lah-mah-sáy-roosh) marshy place
lapa (láh-pah) cave, den
levada (leh-váh-dah) watercourse (see page 6)
lombada (lohm-báh-dah) long ridge
lombo (lóhm-boo) ridge separating two parallel ravines
miradouro (mee-rah-dóh-roo) viewpoint
monte (móhnt) mount
mouro (móor-oo) Moor
nogueira (noh-gáy-rah) nut tree

palheiro (pahl-yáy-roo) cow house thatched cottage
paragem (pah-ráh-jengh) bus stop
paúl (pah-óol) marshland
penha (péyn-yah) rocky hill or cliff
pico (pée-koo) peak
poio (póy-oo) terrace
poiso (póy-soo) pause
ponta (póhn-tah) point
portela (pohr-táy-lah) little gateway
porto (póhr-too) port
prazer (prah-zéhr) pleasure
quebrada (kay-bráh-dah) steep slope
queimada (kay-máh-dah) burnt
rabaça (rah-báh-sah) wild celery
recta (ráy-tah) straight (often a straight stretch of road)
ribeira (ree-báy-rah) river or river valley
risco (réesh-koo) danger
rocha (róh-shah) rock, crag
seixal (sáy-shal) pebbly place
serra (séh-rah) mountain range
sítio (sée-tee-oo) place
torre (tóh-ray) tower
torrinhas (toh-réen-yash) turrets
vale (váhl) valley
vinhático (veen-yáh-tee-koo) indigenous laurel